MW01275305

42 Rules to Turn Your Prospects into Customers

How to Build Profitable Relationships to Close More Sales and Drive More Business

By Meridith Elliott Powell
Foreword by Dr. Ed Brenegar

E-mail: info@superstarpress.com
20660 Stevens Creek Blvd., Suite 210
Cupertino, CA 95014

Published by Super Star Press™, a Happy About® imprint
20660 Stevens Creek Blvd., Suite 210, Cupertino, CA 95014
http://42rules.com

First Printing: October 2010
Paperback ISBN: 978-1-60773-082-8 (1-60773-082-0)
eBook ISBN: 978-1-60773-083-5 (1-60773-083-9)
Place of Publication: Silicon Valley, California, USA
Library of Congress Number: 2010936974

Trademarks

Warning and Disclaimer

Praise For This Book!

"Meridith Elliott Powell offers you the genius of taking the overwhelming and complex and making it clear, simple, and actionable. This is the secret of great coaching; and in her terrific new 42 Rules to Turn Your Prospects into Customers, Meridith provides you with a streamlined, fun, and effective game plan for success. Elevate your confidence and ignite great momentum by reading of Meridith's secrets!"
Brian Biro, America's Breakthrough Coach, Author, *Beyond Success*

"Between the specific action steps and the simplicity of Meridith's ideas, I found myself eager to try what I learned in this benefit-rich book. I gained ideas for my business in almost every chapter and have been effortlessly taking new steps forward with my sales process. Meridith just makes the sales process so easy!"
Misti Burmeister, CEO Inspirion, Inc., New York Times Best-Selling Author, *Boomers to Bloggers: Success Strategies across Generations*

"In today's market, I need all the customers I can get. I wasn't happy with the number of prospects who were slipping through the cracks. Meridith was my missing ingredient. Sales never came easy to me, but Meridith gave me a whole new way to look at the process—a way that fit my personality—a way that I could understand—that actually worked. She didn't just leave me with a strategy on paper—she walked me through it, step by step. There are a lot of books, speakers and coaches out there, and a lot of information to choose from. Meridith gave me that information in a way that made it easy and FUN! Her coaching style is funny, real, and relatable. I highly recommend this book for those who want to turn prospects into customers. The value I gained from Meridith more than made up for the investment."
Kelly Swanson, Comedian and Motivational Speaker, CEO Swanson Speaks, Inc., Author, *Who Hijacked My Fairytale*

"Sales can seem overwhelming and scary to so many, but thank goodness for Meridith. She approaches the topic of sales in a unique way in her new book by laying out easy steps that lead to great relationships that close that deal. This book is ideal for everyone from the sales professional to the professional who never thought they would have to sell. By the time you finish Meridith's book, you will be a salesperson with a smile."

Marquesa Pettway, DTM, Reinvention Expert, Speaker, Author, Coach

Dedication

This is dedicated with love to:

My dear friend Sue, whose wisdom, persistence and unconditional love are the reason this book and so many of my dreams have come true.

My husband Rob, whose passion for life and unwavering support and dedication to me have inspired me to reach new heights.

My mother, whose loving guidance and relentless insistence her children always be gracious, kind, and well-mannered, created the original rules that are the foundation for this book.

Acknowledgments

There are so many individuals I want to thank for helping me write this book. Many wonderful people have taught and mentored me, created amazing experiences with me, and shared research, ideas, and their wisdom unselfishly with me. While I will never be able to name them all, I want to give special thanks to: Rob Powell, Joan McShane, Beth Brand, Sue Fazio, Mary Beth Shera, Melissa Stanz, Pam Lewis, Tim Burleson, Onae Fazio, Kelly Johnson, Marquessa Pettaway, Misti Burmeister, my friends at NSA Carolinas, friends at NSA, Jeff Ward and the "original" team at First Citizens Bank, Ed Brenegar, John Locke, Brian Biro, Keith Challenger, Bill Kelley, Dana Stonestreet, Linda Burwell, Brian Mansfield, Candy Harper, Mark Bennett, and the very talented Patty King. Thanks also to my long list of wonderful clients and the wonderful young mentors in my life, Cabell Brand, Clay Grant, Mason Grant, Mary Kent, and Camryn Wolff.

Epigraph

"Efficiency is doing things right; effectiveness is doing the right things."
Peter Drucker

C o n t e n t s

Contents

Contents

Foreword by Dr. Ed Brenegar

You are about to devour a book written by a wise, passionate, generous expert. Meridith Powell is the gold standard of sales trainers, coaches, and consultants. The reason...she understands, better than most, that the relationship between you and your client or customer is central to success. In addition, she has a methodology for helping you learn to master it. It isn't just a good idea, but an approach that works.

There are lots of people who can teach you to trick people into buying stuff they don't want. Meridith, in this wonderful little book, gives you a way to build a sustainable business through sustainable business relationships. It is a book that you read once, and then again and again and again. You will turn back to Meridith's insights time and time again because she provides answers to questions that we all have.

I love this little book because now all the bits and pieces of wisdom that I've been receiving from Meridith for as long as I've known her are in one place. And you are the beneficiary.

Take your time. Think about what she says. Take notes. Do the tasks that she suggests. Talk about what you are learning with colleagues. Read the book together. You'll find your life and work transformed. I wish you every success as you do.

Thank you very much, and enjoy!

Dr. Ed Brenegar

Dr. Ed Brenegar is a leadership coach, strategist and guide, who helps his clients navigate and succeed in the challenges and opportunities of their professional and personal lives. He owns Circle of Impact Leadership Guide Services and Community of Leadership LLC.
http://www.edbrenegar.typepad.com

Preface

Some people are born to sell! It is as if something in their DNA just resonates with the challenge and opportunity that selling offers. For the rest of us, it's another story! For years, I found sales uncomfortable, unfulfilling, and even a little scary. In every job I had, sales training, sales systems, and sales tracking were all provided... along with plenty of accountability. I had bosses who would make sure I stuck to the program. There was painstaking progress, but the continual struggle made me yearn for the day when I did not have to do this anymore.

Of course, that day never came. Year after year, my dissatisfaction made me ponder: there must be a better way. I laugh to myself now when I hear people say, "Sales is not in my job description;" or "I am going to hire someone to sell for me." I can truly relate; I tried every excuse, but pretending we are not in the business of sales doesn't work. The reason? Selling is a part of life. Whether you have a job, a family, or volunteer in a community, you have to sell. At its core, sales is nothing more than getting people to "buy in" to whatever it is you offer—an idea, a product, a new direction. If you seek a job, encourage a child, start a new program at church, or simply plan a family outing, sales comes into play. You will have to "sell" your idea; you have to understand the value and share your idea in a way that convinces people to participate. Doing that is sales!

So, if selling is a natural part of life, why is it so uncomfortable? The answer, I discovered, is rooted in where the sales profession went wrong. Somewhere along the line books, programs, and techniques began to emerge that made selling far more about helping yourself and your company than serving your customer. Ideas were introduced that promoted aggressive cold-calling techniques, new ideas on how to "close," and how to "up-sell" a customer. Unfortunately, they all shifted the focus from customer-centric selling to me-centric selling.

No wonder we all started to dislike selling! This new style pushed us too far out of our comfort zone, and left us unclear about how to help our customers. Ironically, I watched as my co-workers fought the idea of our organization creating a sales culture; yet daily, I observed them in their personal lives selling everything under the sun. I watched as they convinced their friends to try new restaurants, their children to read more books, and their friends to volunteer. So, what was different? Why were they fighting this idea of being salespeople at work, but embracing sales in their everyday lives?

Because they didn't think they were selling; they thought they were helping. With this paradigm shift, you begin to discover the key to your natural sales style. What I observed was the reason and the way in which they were selling were radically different from what they had been taught to do professionally. The technique they used in their everyday life was rooted in a deep desire to help people, to share information and ideas, whereas the style they used professionally was not their own, but someone else's process.

From this observation, the idea for a new way—my way to sell—emerged. I began to use sales techniques that felt natural for me. Every technique is customer-oriented, with a focus on value, service, and a long-term relationship. I studied everything I could about relationships, networking, and customer service and connected it all to the sales process. The more I adopted my own natural style, the more successful I became. Sales became fun, easy and effective. The more successful I became, the more others sought me out to ask what I was doing. I not only had a strong book of clients, but I looked happy! People would ask me about networking, sales, and building relationships. The number one question on everyone's mind is: "How do you turn a prospect into a customer?"

Thus, the idea for this book! I was asked this question so often that I began to take notes, which turned into a blog, which became this book and my methodology. This book is the culmination of years of experimentation, practice, and hard work, to ultimately find my better way! It is a step-by-step approach of how I found my natural sales style.

I am on a mission; I want to help people learn to love selling. Why? Because I believe with the right approach, you too can find your sales voiceand desire to sell. Selling is both science and art, and you need both: necessary processes (the science), and a natural technique (the art). The consistency of process will give you enough turns at bat, but the sale will come from the passion your customers feel emanate from you.

Read this book, follow these rules, and uncover your natural sales style!

Welcome! I am on a mission to help people learn to love to sell. I want to show you that sales can be fun and rewarding. Like so many of you, I started out hating sales. It was stressful, and something I felt forced to do. Then I realized it was stressful because I followed a set of rules that took the value and the fun out of the process. So I decided to write my own rules, and I discovered my love for sales! Now I want to share these rules with you, so you too can enjoy turning your prospects into customers.

This book is divided into three parts, each representing an important process in approaching prospects and turning them into customers.

Part I is The Foundation. It contains everything you need to consider before you go on your first sales call. I will walk you through every step and encourage you along the way. When you finish this section, you'll actually look forward to setting up a sales call, and you'll be eager to get started on your strategy.

Part II is The Call, your first visit with a potential customer. We will address how to use the foundation rules, and how to engage your customer so you design a sales experience that is positive for both of you.

Part III is The Follow-Up. These rules are so much more than just a thank-you card or a phone call; these are the rules that complete the movement of prospect to customer. They provide the opportunities to offer additional services to an already satisfied customer base, and to solidify relationships and retain business for the long term. A well-executed follow-up process will create a strategy strong in repeat business and referrals.

Who can benefit from my Forty-Two Rules? Anyone! Whether you are the owner of a thriving firm hoping to expand into new territory, or an entrepreneur looking to carve a niche in a competitive market, these rules will give you a blueprint for success.

Sales can be scary. I get that—I've felt that way myself. It's not so overwhelming when it's broken down into just forty-two rules that anyone can learn. This book will leave you brimming with confidence and information.

The real beauty of this book is that you can use it as a template for every prospect. You can run quickly through the headings of this book and ask yourself, "Have I followed each rule for *this* client?"

"What if I'm already in sales?" you ask. "My smart phone is filled with appointments. I'm already making plenty of calls."

That's great! But are you just making calls and taking orders? Are you really learning about your customers? Are you listening to them? Are they engaged enough to confide their needs? These are some of the skills that can make a difference when your business or industry is hit by new competition, price hikes, or changing market conditions. These rules ensure your customers take advantage of all that you have to offer, and you retain their business when the competition calls.

Whether you are new to sales and secretly dreading your sales quota, or a successful sales associate with a scrolling list of appointments, my Forty-Two Rules can show you ways to deepen **and** widen your sales channels. You'll discover a wealth of confidence, expertise, and empathy that you didn't even know you had.

Let's get started!

Part I
The Foundation

In this first section, you'll learn how to prepare to meet your prospect for the first time. The alpha rule to successful selling is confidence, and confidence stems from doing your research. I can't say it often enough: research, research, research!

You'll find that taking time to research your prospect and the potential sale is a path to success. This research will set you up as an expert in your field. It will enable you to give the customer value during your initial visit, such as free information or useful connections. You'll identify small opportunities to serve your customer and demonstrate that you have more to offer than the competition. When your customer feels confident in you, it's easy to feel confident in yourself.

The rules and stories in this book are true and are taken from my years of working as a coach, trainer, and business development expert. They present a guide, a powerful, systematic step-by-step process to help you turn your prospects into customers and ultimately turn those customers into champions. You'll not only learn how to sell, you'll learn how to think like a salesperson: think like someone who knows how to find opportunities, solutions, and new ideas to help prospects and clients get more value from their relationships.

- Rule 1: Rules Are Meant to Be Broken
- Rule 2: Confidence Is Key to Sales
- Rule 3: Target the Right Client
- Rule 4: Know Your Value
- Rule 5: Build Relationships
- Rule 6: Plan Your Success
- Rule 7: Learn to Serve
- Rule 8: Be Prepared to Go the Distance
- Rule 9: Expand Your Brand
- Rule 10: Become a Master Networker
- Rule 11: Create a Communication Line
- Rule 12: Add Value Immediately

1 Rules Are Meant to Be Broken

Thank goodness!

One reason I love and am passionate about sales, marketing and building relationships is that it is far more of an art than a science. Selling is easy, but it is not simple. The process is never black and white, and long-term successful sales-people know that the more flexibility they bring to the process the more successful they are going to be. This is one rule you need to adopt and learn. Each sales situation is different and everyone you sell to is unique. Your attitude, your confidence, and your relationship skills will do so much more to determine your success than the actual steps you take. Understand that first, and you are on the road to being a sales super-star.

As you learn a new approach to sales through this book, I also encourage you to think about yourself. The most important asset in the sales process is you! Determine which rules work best for you, which feel most comfortable, and take the liberty to change and enhance any of these rules. Make this book work for you. Truly think of this book as much as an opportunity to learn about sales as it is an opportunity to learn about yourself.

Years ago I learned that if I wanted to be suc-cessful at sales, I needed to learn to adjust. Just like no two people are alike, no two sales calls, sales cycles, or closings are alike. After all, people buy from people and people sell to people. The situations, the personalities and the goals are always different. So you need to learn to adjust your style as well as the rules you use. For example, the rules I apply when selling to a Fortune 500 company may differ from the rules I apply when working with a start-up organization.

Some of the following rules you may already know; some you will be effective at implementing, and others will be new to you. Perhaps some are steps you have avoided as they take you out of your comfort zone. I encourage you to identify the specific rules that need your focus and work. If time and energy are spent in learning those rules, then you will see a dramatic impact on your overall results.

Enjoy *42 Rules to Turn Your Prospects into Customers*. Learn some new things, implement some new ideas, and break whatever rules you need to make this process, and this book, work for you! This book will not only show you how to enhance your sales skills, but how to think more effectively in sales situations. That will give you the confidence and ability to be successful, no matter the sales situation.

Over the course of your sales career the economy will change, your competition will change, and your prospects and customers will change, but the underlying rules and principles of how to sell, and how to sell effectively, remain the same. Invest in learning these fundamental rules, and you will always find your prospects delighted to turn into your customers!

Confidence Is Key to Sales

Confidence is the first building block you need in your sales foundation. Ask yourself these questions:

- Do I believe in the value of the product or service I sell?
- Do I believe in myself?

Your answers to these questions should be "yes" if you hope to successfully turn your prospects into customers. You can easily build your confidence by following the steps in this rule. No one starts out with confidence; it is something you develop. It stems from learning and investing in yourself, preparing for meetings and sales calls, and taking small risks. Each time you invest in yourself, your confidence builds. While it can be a slow process, once built, it stays with you and transfers into all aspects of your life. It is powerful!

Confidence and personal belief are at the core of successful sales. Do you need to build your confidence? Try these simple steps and watch your confidence grow:

Get a clear vision of what you want.
Sit down and figure out what it is that you want and write it down. Then read it out loud first thing every morning. Yes, you heard me: out loud! Confident people are clear about what they want and they can easily articulate it. There is not a right or wrong vision; there is just **your** vision.

Study and learn.
Devote time each day to reading, studying, and learning. Consistency is the key. Limit your time to thirty minutes or an hour at most. (I have found that introverts will study too long, and extroverts will lose interest if there is not a time limit.) Information and knowledge give you new perspectives, new ideas, and motivation to create solutions.

Learn to fail.
Shift your thought process when it comes to rejection or lost opportunity. If you are not failing, you are not risking enough. Grab failure as an opportunity to grow and learn. Instead of focusing on the failure, focus on what you could do differently or what you have learned. The thing about failure is that no one cares about your failure except you; everyone but you expects you will occasionally fail. Focusing on negative emotion is a waste of your precious energy.

Think positive.
This is easier for some than others. However, everyone has the ability to "catch" negative thoughts and turn them into positive thoughts. Start your day by saying ten positive things about yourself. Again, write them down, post them, and say them out loud every morning. Never underestimate the idea that thought promotes action, and action promotes results.

Reward yourself.
Be kind to yourself. For every little thing that you do well, pay yourself a compliment. You are making a change; you are growing. Positive reinforcement is critical. If you made ten sales calls this week, treat yourself to some small pleasure that you enjoy. If you only made one, compliment yourself on that one and decide on a reward for next week when you meet your goal.

Avoid negative people.
Our belief system is shaped by those with whom we spend the most time. We do not even realize that the negative messages we take in throughout the day are shaping our thoughts, our actions, and our results. Change your negative crowd, your negative television shows, your negative reading materials, and you will change your belief system.

If you believe in yourself, your abilities, and your product, you will not only be able to sell, but you will also be passionate about it. Confidence is key to sales. Build your confidence, and your prospects will turn into customers!

3

Target the Right Client

To turn prospects into clients, you must first be clear about the following:

- With whom am I looking to develop business relationships?
- Why am I looking for them?
- Where am I looking for them?

Here's a newsflash: not everyone wants to buy your product or service. Not everyone can benefit from or pay for your product or service. And not everyone needs it. So your objective is to clearly identify and understand the type of prospect that has the highest likelihood of buying from you. Ask yourself:

- Who needs my product or service?
- Who is able to pay for my product or service?
- With whom do I have the best opportunity of building a relationship?

If you sat down right now and described your perfect customers, you would find they fit a very distinctive niche. There are specific things about these individuals that attract them to your product. The more you can discover this niche, the more you will identify who truly wants what you are selling. Imagine a sales process where you spend the majority of your time working with prospects that actually want and need what you are selling.

Defining your target market is a fun exercise. Consider things like:
- Gender
- Age range
- Hobbies
- What they like to do
- Where they live
- What their interests are
- What they like about you
- Things that are important to them
- What their values are
- What motivates or drives them
- What magazines they like to read
- What movies they like to see
- What products they like to buy

There is no end to what you can identify. Gather as much information as you can, and find out what your ideal clients have in common.

One of my clients, Melissa Lewis, has grown her business quickly and efficiently based on this idea. Every quarter, she updates her Target Market description. She is constantly tweaking, changing, and adding information to her client data. Melissa knows that her ideal clients are successful men between the ages of 45 and 55, professionally driven, well educated (Master's Degree and above), athletic and dedicated to physical fitness, married with high school and college-aged children, and demanding. They also value success, their reputations, their families, and career advancement, and they choose to slow down rather than to retire.

Where does she find these prospects? She knows her prospects are active, so she finds them at professional associations and sporting events. By joining in and participating in these events, she has a very natural way to meet, connect, and build relationships with her prospects. She has also learned why they choose her: because of her effectiveness, accountability, and drive. So she makes sure to emphasize those qualities when making new proposals. Needless to say, even in a changing economy, she has a thriving business and a constant influx of new clients.

If you want to get results quickly and make the most efficient use of your time, then you need to intimately know the type of customer you want to attract.

4

Know Your Value

If you want to turn your prospects into customers, then you must understand what you are selling. In most cases, the product or service that you offer is something that your existing clients can purchase anywhere. So, why should they buy this product or service from you? Gathering and understanding this information is important in your efforts to turn prospects into customers.

So where do you start? Begin by doing a little research. Spend some time interviewing and talking with your existing clients: both those who buy from you often and those who you wish did more business with you.

Discover what they value about you, your product, and your service. Ask questions like:

- Why specifically do you buy from me?
- What specific problems do I solve for you?
- What do I deliver that keeps you coming back?
- What else could I do that would be of value to you?

It may seem awkward at first, but remember that this is simply a way to let your existing clients open up. They will see that you want to serve them better, and that you want to understand what is important to them and what they need and value. This will not only help you gather the information you need; it will also work as a strong retention strategy. Your existing clients will not only be willing to help you, they'll derive increased value from the fact that you are interested in and act on their opinions.

Next, you need to talk with your prospects and really listen. Determine what particular problems or challenges they are facing today. Then spend some time alone or with a friend brainstorming and defining how your product or service adds value, solves problems, and is unique from your competitors'. Once you know this information, you can craft a message that distinguishes the unique aspects of your product or service in the marketplace. This information will help you better connect with your prospects and your customers, and you'll gain credibility as someone who has ideas and solutions.

I have worked with Mark Elliott in Washington, D.C. He uses this strategy routinely in his legal practice, and in doing so, he brings in new business and deepens his existing client relationships. Elliot has learned his clients are always looking to grow their businesses and enhance their networks. So, he recommends that his clients and prospects meet one another for mutual business gain. In other words, he knows from listening to his clients that his high quality legal work is an expectation; he then adds value by acting above and beyond this expectation. His clients may feel they can get high quality legal work most anywhere, but it is Elliot's ability as a connector and a resource that keeps his clients working exclusively with him. The value he provides creates a much easier transition from prospect to client.

If you want to turn your prospects into customers, you must first understand how you are unique from your competitors and why your clients truly buy from you. Then share this unique message with your prospects to help them understand why working with you is the best option.

5 Build Relationships

Turning your prospects into customers is truly all about the "soft" skills: the ability to connect with people, listen, communicate, understand, convey trust, and develop confidence. We call this "building relationships."

If you doubt the validity of investing time and energy in a relationship, then think about this: the chances that you will connect with someone at the exact time that they are ready to buy your product or service are pretty slim. By building the relationship, you are working to ensure that prospects automatically think of you when they are ready to buy.

Those of you who are masters at this already know that you have to start building relationships well before you need the sale. Make no mistake, to be effective at turning your prospects into customers you have to understand that the sales cycle is long. Additionally, you must be aware that the consumer is in control at all times. And here is the reason why: your prospects have the opportunity to buy anything they want wherever, whenever, and from whomever they please.

So where do you start? Well, let's start with the definition of "relationship." According to Webster's Dictionary, relationship is "an emotional connection between two people." For me, I take that definition one step further and say it is an emotional connection between two people, in which each person derives value and feels trust.

To build a relationship like that you have to get to know people. I would argue that you even need to get to know them outside of your business environment. Give them a chance to connect with you, and you with them, on a professional and personal level.

This leads us right back to Rule 3: Target the right client.

I have a client named Martha Poole. She specializes in selling high-end real estate, and she loves golf, horses, and travel. Her passions, both professional and personal, fit together perfectly. She is a member of several country clubs, and she is quite active in the community of people who enjoy horses, both for riding and showing. Through both of these activities, she has met several individuals who share her passion for travel. The shared interests and time spent together make building relationships an easy and enjoyable process.

Naturally, when those individuals want to buy or sell real estate, or if they have friends who want to buy or sell real estate, where do you think they turn? They contact their friend Martha, who is easy to find at the golf course, the riding stables, or at the local horse show. Similarly, once Martha has developed the relationship and built trust, she can ask for business... and she does! Again, after she has built the relationship and established trust, she lets her friends know what she does for a living and that she is looking to grow her business.

If you want to be effective at turning your prospects into customers, like Martha, and if you want to get results, then it is essential that you learn how to build relationships. Invest the time and energy in getting to know people, add value to your business and their lives, and build trust in who you are and the business that you represent.

6 Plan Your Success

To be successful at turning prospects into customers, you need a plan. You need to know specifically where you want to go and how you plan to get there. Years ago I volunteered for a local organization to help raise a large amount of money for a capital campaign. While I had been involved and even led quite a few successful fundraising efforts in our town, I had to admit even I was a little overwhelmed by both the size of this one and the competition we faced. Our campaign chair, luckily for us, was a huge fan of strategic planning. A corporate executive, he had spent years achieving milestones and surpassing goals, all through what he claimed was the power of strategic planning. Again, I was doubtful, but he was so enthusiastic and confident. His leadership, his insistence on investing in a strategic plan, and his dedication to follow through ensured we not only met our goal, we almost doubled it. That day I became a strong believer in the power of having a strategic plan.

Why do strategic plans work? There are a variety of theories, but I believe they work because they provide the framework for common vision, focus, communication, and accountability—all of which help you turn "busy" into "productive."

In business and in life you stand a far better chance of achieving the things you want if you have a plan. There are several ways to design one, and it is important that you find the process that works best for you. I use a method called Systems Thinking Strategic Planning. This approach provides a structure to view each part of your business as integrated systems, which connect to and impact one another. Regardless of the style you choose, here are some tips to help you make this time productive and successful.

Plan.
Annually, block two days for a personal business retreat. I have found that blocking two days ensures a full commitment to completing this critical job.

Use a Model.
Again, a simple google search will uncover a variety of models and methods. I use and am master-certified in Systems Thinking Strategic Planning.

1. Vision, Mission, Core Values, Goals—Where do you want to be?

2. SWOT Analysis (Strengths, Weaknesses, Opportunities, Threats) Where are you now?

3. Strategic Actions: The Journey—Where will you focus to get from current state to fuure state?

4. Outside Impact—What outside forces could positively and negatively impact your plan?

Post.
Post your vision, mission, and core values somewhere prominent so that you read them every day. If you want to achieve it, you need to see it and feel it.

Review.
Review your actions and behaviors each month. Which actions are producing desired results, which are not, and what do you need to change going forward? Try having an "action huddle" every week to review actions and results.

Track and Measure.
Set aside time each quarter to review your whole plan. Again, what is going well, what is not and what, if anything, needs to change? During this meeting, take time to review how many prospects have turned into clients and what impact that has had on the bottom line.

Planning for success is a very critical step in working smarter, more efficiently, and in building your confidence and motivation to achieve your goals. If you want to turn your prospects into customers, then you need to take the time to plan for success!

7 Learn to Serve

Why are you and most people reluctant to sell? This is an interesting question, and one that is key to uncovering the underlying motivation needed to turn prospects into customers. If you want to make money, increase your business, and keep your existing customers, then you must sell. So why do so many people dislike it?

Somewhere along the line, salespeople unfortunately got connected to words such as "pushy," "aggressive," and "confrontational." These are words that make most people understandably cringe. In reality, if you want to turn your prospects into customers, then the last thing you want to be is pushy, aggressive, or confrontational. If you want to turn your prospects into customers, you must first learn to serve. Serving is something that most people like, identify with, and strive to do. Ironically, your ability to serve is directly related to your ability to turn your prospects into customers.

Great service brings great sales! If you care about people, and offer a product or service that you believe is of benefit and value, you can sell and be terrific at it.

Selling is nothing more than the following:

Believe in and know the value of your product or service.
What problem does it solve? Does it save money, provide peace of mind, build confidence, or increase efficiency? You should be able to

articulate not only the features of your product or service, but also what difference it will make to your prospect's life.

Learn to ask questions and really listen.
Who are your clients and what is important to them? What challenges do they face? What opportunities are available to them? Learn to identify what problems they need to solve.

Provide solutions that solve their problems.
Identify what they shared with you about their challenges and opportunities. How can you use this newfound knowledge along with your resources, products, or services to help them see and achieve their goals?

I saw a wonderful example of this philosophy practiced by Sandy Tolbert, a physical therapist in Georgia. Sandy's environment is competitive, and she has to work to retain and increase her referrals from local physicians. I was coaching with Sandy one day, when I observed the following call on a prospect: Sandy set up the call with a local physician from whom she wanted referrals. Understanding that she knew very little about his practice, she began the call, not by talking about what she wanted, but rather focusing on what he wanted. How? She simply asked questions, like "Tell me about your practice. What is going well and what opportunities do you see? What challenges are you facing?" Slowly, the conversation turned towards patients.

Rather than ask for referrals, Sandy continued with questions, "What is most important for you in terms of the referral relationship and care of your patients?" Through asking questions, Sandy not only deepened the relationship with the physician, but she also discovered a list of challenges this physician faced, opportunities he had, and how she could best serve his business. Rather than leaving that office with one opportunity, she left with a variety of ideas, products, and services that she could offer that would speak directly to this physician's needs. This one call led to a series of calls that ultimately built a strong referral relationship between Sandy and this physician.

If you want to turn your prospects into customers, then you must first learn to serve. Invest in understanding your customers by identifying their issues and concerns; take care of their needs first, and learn to sell through service.

8 Be Prepared to Go the Distance

Experts say that in a good economy it takes seven or eight contacts to turn a prospect into a customer. In a tough economy it takes ten to twelve, and in a changing economy that number moves to fifteen or sixteen contacts.

Do you know how many tries the average salesperson attempts before writing off a prospect? The answer is just three or four. If you want to turn your prospects into customers, then you have to realize your business is a marathon, not a sprint!

So how long do you stay in contact and how many attempts do you make before you give up on a prospect? You need to be prepared to go the distance.

If you are in this business for the long haul, then ask yourself how you will stay in contact with prospects. Clearly define your process for turning a prospect into a customer.

Keep in mind that most of your competition is giving up after just three or four tries. So if you continue to proactively cultivate the relationship, when the prospect decides to buy, it probably will be from you.

My husband's dental office practices this "marathon method" every day in their office. When patients first visit, they start off with a welcome tour of the office. Patients meet the full staff, and they discuss their needs and expectations with the hygienist and the dentist. The hygienist and the dentist take notes as they listen, and they work with the patient to develop a plan. They then review the information with the patient, and ask the patient how he or she would like to move forward. They suggest to the patient which dental work is critical and discuss other recommendations for good preventative care. The patient gets to decide how to proceed, based on his or her time constraints, financial plans, and goals. The dentist and hygienist will provide input and feedback, but the patient ultimately chooses how to proceed.

The bottom line is that the patient receives value from sharing concerns and receiving input; and by having his or her critical issues handled, the patient understands all available options and chooses what, when, and how to move forward. The result in this office varies: some patients want care immediately; others come back in six months, one year, or sometimes two years to receive care. The patients are happy because they receive the necessary care and information to take care of their teeth, and the decisions about when and how to move forward are theirs, fitting their time and their budget. This dental team understands that the patient is in control. They understand how to balance quality care with patient needs. They understand that this is a marathon, not a sprint.

Right from the start you have to be willing to go the distance with your prospects. Each interaction with a prospect or client is an opportunity to move the relationship forward. You serve as a guide and a resource by asking questions, providing solutions, and creating opportunities for your prospect to become your customer. It is ultimately your prospect's decision when, where, and how to become your customer. By running this marathon, you can ensure that when your prospect is ready to buy, you will be first on the list.

9

Expand Your Brand

The idea that actions speak louder than words comes into play as you work to turn prospects into customers. Everything about you conveys a message: how you introduce yourself, how you dress, and how you keep in touch with prospects. Whether you realize it or not, you are telling prospects if you are trustworthy, how you can add value, and if you are worth their time.

In a world where trust and value have become the new Return on Investment (ROI), your personal brand is as important as the product or service that you sell. You have to be as good at marketing yourself as you are at selling your product or service.

Remember, competition is fierce and growing stronger every day. Consumers have a million choices about where, when, how, and from whom they buy a product. If you want to be the one turning prospects into customers, then you better be the first one that they think of when they are ready to act on their needs. That takes marketing: you need awareness, top-of-mind connection, a keep-in-touch strategy, and a highly regarded reputation.

A big part of this strategy is your personal brand, not your company's brand. You need to build a personal brand that is powerful and strong.

Your personal brand is all about how you position yourself in the marketplace. How you look, what you say, and how you act are part of the client's experience when interacting with you. This includes how well you listen, communicate, and follow up.

When we go to the doctor, we expect a clean atmosphere, white coats, well trimmed hair, and a sterile environment. If our doctor walked in with dirty fingernails, slightly messed up hair and and untucked shirt, then we would run, not walk, out of there. However, a mechanic sporting this look makes us feel we are in the hands of someone who has been under the hood and knows what they are doing. These professionals have a brand; and if you want to turn your prospects into customers, then you must have a brand, too.

So how do you develop a personal brand? For starters, you already have one. It may or may not be the one that you want, but you do have one. A great exercise is to make a list of ten competencies, or ten ways you want people to describe you. Then ask yourself how you measure up. Would your prospects and customers describe you this way? If not, how can you be proactive in conveying this message?

Try keeping a list of your ten competencies on your desk. Read them out loud every morning. Over time you will have gained a reputation that matches your list. It is simply about focus! Having a strong brand and distinct reputation is a major asset in your ability to turn your prospects into customers.

So the next time you're heading out to a networking event, calling on a prospect, or heading to a community meeting, take a moment to stop and think of your personal brand checklist:

- Am I trustworthy?
- Am I positive and upbeat?
- Am I confident?
- Have I prepared for the call or event?
- Do I know what I'm talking about?
- Do I have my customer's best interests at heart?
- Would I hire or work with me?
- Do I look and act professional?

Test yourself. Hold yourself to these standards, and constantly look to improve, mold, and expand your brand. This provides a huge competitive edge in your goal to turn prospects into customers!

10 Become a Master Networker

People who know how to network know how to turn their prospects into customers. They are always making their goals, closing sales, gaining new customers, and making it all look effortless and stress-free. They have fun!

Allow me to let you in on a little secret: these people simply understand the value of networking and the role that it plays in turning your prospects into customers. I call these people the Master Networkers. They are individuals who have embraced and consistently practiced the art of networking to turn their prospects into customers.

So how do they do it? How do they make it look so easy?

First, they embrace networking as a lifestyle instead of an event. Though it seems simple enough, this is where most people get derailed. For most of us, networking is simply a task, something we mark off a checklist. In reality, however, a successful networker recognizes this process as a skill, something you learn and consistently perfect! To truly master the art, you have to embrace it as part of who you are and the way you live.

Secondly, they network first to serve others. The Master Networkers understand that they are capable of developing a bank of people who can work together for the benefit of everyone. They approach networking with a servant's heart, ask questions to learn about their networking partners, and keep in touch to build the relationships.

If you approach each day and each event as an opportunity to connect with and add value to those you meet, and to add value to your relationships, then good things start to happen. You encounter many interesting people, and you begin to build a reputation as someone people need to know and want to know. You become a person who is well-connected, is "in the know," and is a valuable resource. Most importantly, however, you become someone that people are familiar with and someone that people trust. In today's world and changing economy, a reputation defined by familiarity and trust is a valuable reputation to have.

Meet John Locke, a senior executive with a large foundation. I call John a Master Networker, and he is amazing at building relationships. John really connects with people everywhere he goes and at every event he attends. It is evident by his conversations that he is interested in and cares about people. He asks questions and he listens. He learns about people by finding out what they do, what is important to them, and what they personally need to be successful.

People describe John as the resource of western North Carolina. If you need help, support, or a connection, then John is your guy. What is the result? The foundation he supports is thriving, he serves on the board of directors for several successful organizations, and continually has his pick of career and job opportunities. While other organizations struggle to raise funds, and many individuals are unable to find jobs, John's foundation and his personal marketability remain in demand because people value trust and support authenticity in any economy.

The art of turning prospects into customers begins with the simple step of networking to help others. Let this type of networking become your way of life and sit back to watch good things start to happen, like greater business results, more satisfaction in your profession, and less stress in your life!

11 Create a Communication Line

You need a fast, simple, and memorable way to tell people who you are and what you do. Some people call this an elevator speech: a 30-second description of you. I like the term "communication line" because it better describes what you are doing with this process. You are communicating, sharing information. Simply put, a communication line is a descriptive and concise way of sharing who you are, what you do, what problems you can solve, and what value you can add.

Let's look at an example:

1. Meet Paul Clark, a CPA who does tax and accounting work for small business owners.

2. Meet Paul Clark, a CPA who specializes in making tax and accounting work simple to understand, less stressful, and fun to do.

You can see and actually hear the difference. The first introduction is fine, but it lacks personality. However, the second introduction is more informative, and it is memorable. It puts a smile on your face when you say it.

Why are communication lines so important?
When you meet people, you need a fast and memorable way to introduce yourself. If you give people something meaningful and memorable to talk about, then they will share your information with others. That is the point of a communication line: to give the people you meet a reason to

refer and remember you the next time that they need, or meet someone who needs, your services.

Why are communication lines so short?

Remember, our goal with networking and building relationships is to learn about the other person. A short communication line gets your point across quickly and conveys the information you want without dominating the conversation. If you talk too long, people tune you out, and too much information makes it harder for people to remember the important points. Being concise and informative makes you appear confident, too. Rather than struggling to define who you are and what you do, use your communication line to deliver a smart, quick message that supports your brand.

How do you build your communication line?

This should be easy since you have already determined your value and the problem that you solve. Building your communication line simply takes that information and condenses it into a short statement.

Answer these questions:

1. What is your name and profession?

2. What value do you add?

3. What problem can you solve?

4. What benefit do you provide?

For example:

Name: Meridith Elliott Powell
Profession: Coach, Speaker, Business Development Expert
Value Added: I help people turn their prospects into customers and their customers into champions!
Problem Solved: Learn how to turn your sales anxiety and stress into sales fun and success!
Benefit: Working with me, you'll trade the anxiety and stress of sales for fun and success!

Can I have more than one communication line?

Absolutely! We all have more than one talent, and our talents solve more than one problem. So yes, it is smart to have more than one communication line. I have two or three that I use, depending on the event I am attending and my conversational partner.

If you want to further support your brand image and turn your prospects into customers, then take a few moments and develop a smart, effective communication line.

12 Add Value Immediately

While the economy is changing, the basic rules of selling never change. At the core, sales is about adding value by delivering a service or product to someone who can benefit from what you have to offer. Adding value requires a long-term approach and results in a true relationship. This often creates the opportunity for the customer and the salesperson to work together for many years over the life of the business.

While there are solid salespeople who clearly grasp the concept of adding value, not many understand the power of adding value **immediately**. This means adding value at the beginning of the relationship, long before you ever discuss or get the sale. Why would you "give away" value to someone who may not even buy from you? Remember, we are running a marathon, not a sprint. We are building relationships and leading with a servant's heart to build a brand.

In a fast-paced and ever-changing economy, selling is about building trust and value, and conveying confidence. It is important to understand that people react positively to someone they believe is interested in them and willing to help. Adding value up-front, when you first meet someone, is one of the fastest ways you can convey to your prospect that you will put his or her interests first. It builds trust and shows your prospect that he or she can count on you.

As soon as you make connections with your contacts or prospects, begin to think about how you can help them. Ask questions as you network, and listen to the answers. Determine what individuals need and how you can help.

I observed an excellent example of this while speaking to a group of business owners and entrepreneurs. An organizational development manager, Diane Eller with Carolina Family Eye Care, introduced herself and talked with people before my session started. She stood out because I am always impressed when I see individuals making the most of an opportunity.

After my session, I approached Diane, introduced myself, and told her I admired her networking efforts. As I began to ask her more questions, she shared her list of the people she had met and what little things she could do to help each one. One gentleman was having trouble managing multiple generations of employees; Diane had a great white paper she was willing to send his way. Another was expanding his bank into Maryland; Diane had a colleague who worked for a few companies in that region and had offered to make a few introductions. Another was simply not sure where to get a schedule of events for upcoming programs, so Diane simply gave him hers.

Diane took a few minutes before a seminar session and turned them into a connection experience. She introduced herself to people, asked a few short questions, and compiled a list of how she could help these contacts. Now what did Diane gain from this? She gained contacts that were anxious to hear from her again, and she gained permission to build a relationship with each of these individuals. With small gestures, she was able to differentiate herself from the other consultants at the event; and as you can imagine, her next contact proved to be easy and quite successful.

If you want to turn your prospects into customers, then learn to add value immediately. Listen intently. Find out what people need, and determine how you can help.

Part II
The Call

Now it's time to move on to that important visit, the sales call.

Too many people look at this as a drop-in, a handshake, a chance to leave a brochure and make a quick sales pitch. Is that the kind of thing that impresses you? I thought not.

By following the steps laid out in The Foundation, you've already connected to your prospect. Now understand they're giving you something of value: their time.

In this section, you will learn how to make excellent use of that time.

I will lead you through a step-by-step process to prepare for the sales appointment, and then I will show you how to maximize the face-to-face opportunity. And you'll have fun!

The confidence you acquired in The Foundation will now be put on display. It's so easy: just be honest about your intentions, and state your purpose for the visit and your goal. Since a sales call should be twenty percent talking and eighty percent listening, you don't need to worry about putting on a big production. You can customize your "script" to meet your needs; it can be as

42 Rules to Turn Your Prospects into Customers

simple as, "We sell widgets specifically designed for your industry, and we'd like to learn more about you. We want to know how we can help with your current needs and your future goals."

- Rule 13: Follow the Steps to Set an Appointment
- Rule 14: A Sales Call Is a Privilege
- Rule 15: Do Your Homework
- Rule 16: Define Your Purpose
- Rule 17: Ask Great Questions
- Rule 18: Create a Valuable Support Statement
- Rule 19: Deliver a Strong Close
- Rule 20: Master the Art of Listening
- Rule 21: Learn Your Style
- Rule 22: Solve the Right Problems
- Rule 23: Know Your Competition
- Rule 24: Develop a Passionate Attitude
- Rule 25: Open the Door to Opportunity
- Rule 26: Stop Making Cold Calls
- Rule 27: Structure a Series of Small Call

13 Follow the Steps to Set an Appointment

We have all received this phone call: "Hi, Mr. Smith, this is Susan with XYZ Company. I sell widgets, and I would like to come by and talk with you about how our widgets could benefit you and your company. My phone number is 555-555-5555. Please call me back and let me know a time that would work for you."

What is wrong with an approach like this? Well, it is likely Mr. Smith is a busy man. The fact he does not know or has never met Susan means he will not return her phone call. Since Mr. Smith will not return her phone call, Susan will have to make that uncomfortable call several more times before ever getting an appointment, or she will simply give up.

When calling to set an appointment, your sales success depends on these three steps:

Have a reason to call.
The rules in Part I: The Foundation prepare you to make the call. You know the person on the other end of the phone has a need, can benefit from your product or service, and has expressed interest. This makes picking up the phone much easier and ensures better use of your time and the prospect's time.

Prepare and plan.
No matter how well you think you know a person, you should prepare to make the appointment call. Do your research to learn about the

company and the person you are calling. It is important to know your facts and to ensure that your timing is right.

Here is an example:
After talking with a woman that I met at a networking event, I discovered her company was getting ready to go through a strategic planning process. I made a mental note to follow up with her. Through my research, however, I learned her husband was having surgery, and she would be taking a week off from work. So instead of making phone calls to set up an appointment, I sent her a note expressing my wishes for her husband's speedy recovery. I then followed up two weeks later. She was so appreciative of my gesture, and this connection made talking about business an easy and natural step.

Take control of the call, and set the appointment.
People are busy. They will respect someone who shows interest, has a specific reason to call, and uses their time efficiently. First, understand your confidence level, positive attitude, and enthusiasm are even more important when engaging the prospect on the phone. Second, have a connecting greeting. This is something that conveys you know and understand the prospect. Third, get to the point. State your reason for calling, the benefit you can offer, and the next step to discussing it further.

Here's an example:
"Hi, Tom, this is Meridith Elliott Powell. That sure was a great golf tournament last week, wasn't it? Congratulations again to you and your team on your win. I am calling because I wanted to follow up on our conversation about your goals for next year. I would love to buy you lunch or a cup of coffee early next week so we can finish our discussion."

This example is personable, focused, and effective.

If you follow these steps to setting an appointment, your prospects will welcome your call, look forward to meeting with you, and be far more open to buying your product or service.

14

A Sales Call Is a Privilege

You just completed one of the most important tasks in sales: getting the appointment. Congratulations! This means you have successfully convinced someone—who is likely very busy—to take time out of his day to listen to you talk about your product or service. That is an accomplishment. These days, time is money, and this person has no guarantee that your product or service is going to be interesting or beneficial. Still, you convinced this person to give you something of value, a piece of his or her time.

As a salesperson, you must understand that a sales call is a privilege. All too often salespeople forget that one of the most precious things a business owner has is time. You need to recognize and respect the fact that by agreeing to meet with you, a business owner has given you something of value. Remember that and act accordingly; then your prospect will be grateful and impressed, and you will immediately stand apart from the competition.

If you want to turn your prospects into customers, then plan and prepare for the sales call. Preparation shows clients you respect them and value their time. There are many ways to prepare for a sales call, and any planning style you use is fine, as long as you use one.

I keep my planning and preparation simple, following just five easy steps. The next few rules will look more closely at each step, but for now, a quick overview will demonstrate how they work together.

Do your homework.
Before you ever show up to call on a potential customer, you need to have done your research. Learn as much as you can about your prospect and his or her company. Salespeople often overlook this step, but avoiding it ensures you lack the information on which to build your call.

Set objectives.
Determine your focus, what you want to happen on the call, and how you will know if it is successful. Write your objectives down, making them time-specific, actionable, and measurable. These objectives hold you accountable to moving the call forward.

Ask the right questions.
In a sales call, you should talk twenty percent of the time and listen eighty percent of the time. This is an opportunity to learn your client's perspective on what he wants and needs. He will tell you what to sell if you ask the right questions and listen well. Good questions come from quality research and strong objectives.

Create a support statement.
Once you have spent time listening and thinking about what your prospect has said, it is time to offer a support statement. This statement should be based on what you learned from the questions you asked, and it provides solutions to the prospect's specific challenges or opportunities. Your support statement needs to be timely and relevant in order to make an impact.

Deliver a strong close.
Once you have shared your support statement, give the client an opportunity to take advantage of your offer. Deliver a strong close that relates back to your objectives, and you will keep the sales call moving forward.

Treat a sales call as a privilege. Be thankful for the opportunity you have. By moving the process forward with a structured plan, you will succeed in your efforts to turn your prospects into customers! Rules 15–18 go into each of these ideas in more detail. Read on.

15 Do Your Homework

Once you have set the appointment with your prospect, your first step is preparation. Preparation is important because it sets the tone for the call, and it shows the prospect that you care about him and value his time. When you prepare you ensure that your time together is well spent. In a consistently changing and highly competitive economy, preparation and planning are essential.

Spend a little time researching and finding out about the company, your prospect, and his role in the company. The Internet has made finding information so easy: simply enter key words into a search engine, and your prospect's website, articles written about them, reviews of the company, and interesting information about their competition is at your fingertips. Within just a few moments, you can find out how many employees they have, how long they have been in business, who they do business with, what their goals are, what their financial results have been, and much more. The Internet contains a wealth of information, and by investing a little time, you can easily get the background needed to put together an effective sales plan.

Once you have done the technical research, it is time to do "personality research" on the company and your prospect. Personality research is the information that will allow you to make an emotional connection with your prospect. Buying is emotional, so it is important to connect with your prospects emotionally if you want to turn them into customers.

Again, start with the Internet. You can learn a lot from social networking sites, the prospect's blog, or volunteer work in which they are involved. Then talk with people who know your prospect. They can share information, such as your prospect's preferred method of communication, hobbies, and how he makes decisions. Finding out those key, relevant things will help you to connect with your prospect.

Let me share a great example of a sales professional who failed to do this. She did a wonderful job on the technical research, but she missed a golden opportunity by ignoring the personality research. I actually arranged this call for her; she is a friend of mine who wanted to meet another business owner whom I know well. I offered to introduce the two of them. She followed up, set up the call, and found that he was actually in need of her services. All appeared as if it would go well.

A few days later, I called to see how things were going with the two of them. My friend thought the call went great. She asked good questions, identified a need, and was on her follow-up. However, when I spoke with him, I found out that he felt quite differently. He had just made a difficult decision to run for political office. It had been on the news, in all the papers, and it was an important topic for him. She never mentioned it, and never even asked about his life outside of the business. His interpretation, whether right or wrong, was that she was uninformed and uninterested in him personally. She never got the business, not because he didn't need her product, but simply because she did not do her homework.

If you want to turn your prospects into customers, then you must invest time in learning as much as you can about them before the call. This shows you care and are interested in and respect your prospects enough to spend their time wisely.

16 Define Your Purpose

Sales calls are expensive. According to Allbusiness.com, the average cost of a sales call ranges from $100 to $250, depending on years of experience and salary. Think about that: if the average salesperson makes three calls per day, over the course of a year (allowing for vacations and holidays) that is an annual cost of $75,000–$187,000. If you are investing that much money in making sales calls, shouldn't you ensure that you make money or, more importantly, that you don't lose money? Sales calls yield a high rate of return when they are successful. Without them, you cannot stay in business. However, keep in mind that they are expensive. So if the investment is high, you need to do everything possible to ensure your return on investment is worth the effort. Defining your objectives and purpose before you make a sales call greatly increases the chance that your investment will yield a high rate of return.

Before you make a sales call, you need to know why you want to call. Yes, you want to make a sales call because you want more business, but beyond that, why are you making this call? In other words, what is your goal for making this sales call?

You need to write down your sales call purpose. It needs to be actionable, measurable, and time-specific. Your purpose needs to ensure that you hold yourself accountable to accomplish something and that this purpose moves the sales process forward to the next step.

An easy way to remember the characteristics of a sales call purpose is the acronym S.M.A.R.T. (**S**pecific, **M**easurable, **A**ttainable, **R**easonable, and **T**imely.)

It is important to note your purpose will vary, depending on your given stage of the calling process. For example, if this is your first call to this prospect, your purpose may be to establish rapport, learn more about his business, and gain permission to set up a second call to share information on how your services could benefit him. If this is your third call, then your purpose may be to present the proposal you have prepared, gain the prospect's feedback and input, and have the prospect commit to act on the proposal within thirty days. In both examples, the purpose is written, specific, measurable, attainable, reasonable, and timely. It is important to note that both situations require prior thought about how to structure the call so that you can achieve your purpose in a natural and comfortable way.

Because I never know how a sales call will go until I am actually on the call, I always have two, or sometimes three, purposes written down. My first purpose is my "mini-purpose," and if on the call I realize that this prospect is going to need time (meaning I need to build the relationship first, or create the need, or prove the value) to move to the next level, then I will work towards achieving this first purpose. If the call seems to be going a little better than I expected, I have established a good rapport, and their answers are revealing needs that fit my services, then I may move to my second purpose. Then just for fun, I always write down a third "go for it" kind of purpose. You know every once in a while, you meet a prospect and you just hit it off. The call goes like clockwork. Well, even though those times are few and far between, I find that I am better prepared and able to grab the opportunity if I have created my third and highest purpose. By pre-stating two or three purposes, you are prepared with questions and research to meet the needs and provide solutions for whatever your prospects want.

A stated purpose ensures you are always working towards moving the relationship forward and closer to a sale. **Remember, a sales call is a privilege, and defining your purpose shows that you respect your prospects and value their time!**

17 Ask Great Questions

Asking questions is a lost art in sales, networking, and general conversation. If you want to be great at sales, if you want to turn your prospects into customers, then you need to ask great questions. Be curious. Take an interest, and have a desire to learn all about your prospect. There is gold in the answers that you receive!

There are so many benefits to asking your prospects great questions. First, people love to talk about themselves. When you ask questions, you present an opportunity to do just that, and you accomplish a major step in the sales process: emotional connection. If you talk about yourself and your company, you will bore the prospect and he will lose interest.

Second, asking great questions allows the prospect to open up, giving you information about his preferred time and manner of doing business. If you listen closely, he'll share his biggest challenge, tell you how he makes decisions, and tell you whom your biggest competition is.

So how do you know the right questions to ask? While researching, simply write down the questions that come to your mind. You will find details of the company's annual report and information on their product lines, major clients, and executives' backgrounds.

You can then use your interview to uncover things like:

- How is the current economy impacting this company financially, strategically, and from a moral standpoint?
- What opportunities is the company creating?
- What opportunities are being lost?
- What issues are most critical to focus on in the next year?
- Which best practices and strategies are working for the company right now?
- What is one thing about the company that needs to change in the next year?
- Who is the company's competition, and how well do they compete?

The list goes on. The point is that if you ask questions and listen, the prospect will tell you exactly what is wrong and what solution they are looking for. In other words, your prospect will tell you exactly how to present a solution that will ensure a sale. All you have to do is ask questions.

At a sales and networking workshop I gave in North Carolina, a personal trainer and member of my audience named Nancy approached me. She needed to grow her client base, retain more customers, and increase her number of referrals. Along with the other strategies we reviewed in the workshop, we discussed her sales process. Here is what we discovered: While she asked her prospects and customers the usual questions (what brought them to her, how they discovered her; what their goals were, etc.), she was not really connecting with them. She needed to ask better and deeper questions, so we added questions. What did they like and not like about fitness and nutrition? What positive changes would a fitness program bring to their lives? What did they consider to be success? How did they like to be supported and motivated?

Based on what we learned about her current customer base and her target market, we created questions that would get the clients to open up and share their wants, needs, and struggles. Nancy was then able to design more personal fitness plan presentations and training programs that made sure the client received exactly what he desired in terms of training, support, and information.

Asking great questions is fun, interesting, and crucial in the sales process. If you want to turn your prospects into customers, then take the time to develop and ask great questions.

18 Create a Valuable Support Statement

The purpose of a sales call is to get more business, but it is also an opportunity to learn about a business and the people running it. I find it so interesting how and why business owners got their start, how they run their business, and how they make their business successful. The sheer guts, creativity, and innovation it takes to run a business is always inspiring.

The research, purpose, and question rules of a sales call show you, a salesperson, where, when, and how you can help the business owner. This rule, the support statement, is where you transition into how your product or service can help your prospect be more successful.

To deliver a good support statement, you need to shift your thinking. The call is about your prospect, not about you. You should set up a sales call to learn about what particular opportunities and challenges face your prospect's business and if your product or service could be of benefit. From this process, you discover opportunity. This opportunity is your support statement.

Discovery is key.
You cannot really plan a support statement ahead of time. You need to ask great questions and listen to the prospect talk first. Through this conversation, you will discover how and why your product or service could specifically benefit this prospect. If you have done great research and developed a strong purpose, you may have

some ideas in place, but in order to deliver a solid support statement, your ideas should come directly from your conversation with the prospect.

Connection is your credibility.
By connecting the support statement directly to what the prospect just told you, your credibility increases. He knows that you were listening. He knows that you care, and he believes you want to help. You make the call about him and not about you.

Involvement is access.
If you involve the prospect in the support statement, he is far more open to your suggestions and ideas. Clarify the problem or challenge you believe you heard, to be sure you got it right. Then state what you believe he wants the outcome to be and ask for confirmation. Finally, offer your solution (product/service) to help your prospect reach his goal.

For example, this was my support statement earlier this year when calling on a travel industry executive in regards to her selling strategy: "Jen, thank you for sharing so much information with me. You have given me great responses to my questions. There is a lot we can do together. First, let me clarify, just to make sure that I understand you correctly. Your biggest challenge right now, as you are new in your role, is motivating and supporting your sales team in this competitive environment. Is that correct? Great! Now, while you feel you have an exceptional team, you don't feel they've had the support of proper training and clear objectives. This is all new to you because this team just came under your supervision. Your primary focus is marketing and public relations. Is that right? Terrific! Thank you. I would love to discuss a few ideas and suggestions of how to approach this challenge. Some tools and techniques I feel would be perfect for you and help you more than achieve your objective." The call then continued from there.

If you want to turn your prospects into customers, then you need to transition to the sale with a meaningful support statement.

Deliver a Strong Close

I often wonder how many articles and books exist to help salespeople "close the deal"—as if there is a magic phrase or secret way to ensure that the prospect signs on the bottom line. Let me assure you there is not! Engage the prospect, listen, and add value. That is how you close a sales call.

Turning your prospects into customers is about creating long-term relationships. You must do your research, define your purpose, ask great questions, and transition into the sale with a meaningful support statement. If you do not plan ahead of time and structure the sales call correctly, then closing the call will be extremely difficult. Nevertheless, even if you do things well, you still do have to ask for the business. You still have to close the sale.

So how do you deliver a strong close? First, you have to understand that turning a prospect into a customer is actually a series of small closes, not just one big close. Prospects need time to get to know you, especially today, when trust, value, and personal connection are increasingly important. You also need time to prove that you deserve and want the business.

The close should be based on and tied to your purpose, and tied to the pace of the prospect. That is why we always go into a sales call with two or three stated purposes. Observing the pace of the prospect and listening for clues is how you decide how to close the call. What "level" of close do you feel best fits this prospect? Setting the right pace and choosing the right purpose build trust with the prospect. For example, if your purpose is to schedule a second meeting and present a proposal on how you can save the prospect money in his banking services, then scheduling a second meeting is your close for this call. If your purpose is to have your prospect discuss and commit to the proposal, then your close is to gain their commitment and set an engagement start date. Your purpose should tie directly to your close!

Second, your close needs to be a balance of respect and assertiveness, a balance that will move the sales call forward. If you ask for too much, then the prospect may think your sole interest lies in what you stand to gain; you must connect the close to your purpose and what your prospect has told you. If you avoid the close altogether, then you risk not closing the sale and looking foolish in front of the prospect. They expect you to ask for business. Prospects want to work with confident people, and by asking for their business, you show you intend to work hard for them.

Third, if your prospect says no, then embrace it! This only means that you did not create enough value or benefit for the prospect to want to do business with you right now. Learn from this and work at developing value so that you will have a chance with this prospect again. You never know what is going on in their world. Often, people will say no because the timing is wrong. Learn from rejection, and use it to improve your future calling efforts.

Yes, the close is key to turning prospects into clients; however, if you follow the rules and invest in adding value, your prospects will close the sale for you. All you have to do is ask!

20 Master the Art of Listening

Recently, I participated in an online discussion entitled, "What do you feel is the most important part of a sales call?" Some said the success of a call depended on the opening; others said the close of a sales call determined its success; and still others said a call was successful if the client said yes. There was a lot of good information, but it seemed a silly discussion. Is one part of a sales call really more important than the others?

As I sat and thought about this discussion, the idea of listening kept coming to mind. I am not going to say that listening is the most important part of a sales call, but you will miss the advice of your client if you don't listen.

You know your sales call is going well when the client is doing most of the talking, responding to the great questions you asked. Remember the talking to listening percentages: twenty percent and eighty percent, respectively. **If you ask great questions and listen well, the prospect will provide you with opportunities to help you sell your product or service.** Prospects don't want you to tell them what they want before you understand their problem. Instead, they want to share their story and hear your ideas about how you can benefit them.

So how do you become a great listener? How do you convey to the client that you hear what they are saying?

Know your communication style.
Listening well is a critical part of communication. Understand the strengths and weaknesses of your natural style, and discover what needs work. Be self-aware, and own the responsibility of adjusting your style to better connect with others.

Learn what to do and what not to do from others.
Dedicate a day to watching people you interact with, and observe whether they listen to you. You will learn more from this process than from any advice I can give on how to be a great listener.

Engage your whole body.
Make eye contact with the prospect and use facial expressions as they talk. If they say something amusing, smile. If they are conveying serious information, look interested. If they are saying something that you agree with, nod your head. Engaging more than just your ears will help you pay attention and will let the prospect know you are listening.

Practice.
Your listening skills will improve with practice. Spend ten minutes talking with a family member, friend, or your children, and just listen. When they are finished, try to repeat what you believe you heard. It's fun, and you'll improve your listening skills. Your conversational partner will also feel more valued.

Do not interrupt.
Nothing is more distracting than interruption. No matter how great your advice is, interrupting the prospect shows that you do not value what he is saying. I read somewhere that this is called "topping." You just can't wait to jump in and "top" what the other person is saying. This causes you to fail to listen.

Take action.
The most powerful part of listening takes place long after the interaction. People know they were heard when you take action on what they said.

Listening is so essential, and it is consistently listed as one of the key ways people are made to feel important, cared about, and valued. The prospect feels valued by having been heard, and the sales professional gains the exact information needed to move the call forward. If you want to turn your prospects into customers, and make selling easy and fun in the process, then learn to listen.

Learn Your Style

I have heard it said that merely fifteen percent of our success in life relates to a technical skill. This means that the skills we spend our youth, college years, and early adult life honing only account for a small portion of our success. The other eighty-five percent comes from our ability to communicate and connect with others.

Your ability to communicate is a powerful asset in your ability to sell. A successful sale is all about connection, emotion, and the ability to communicate. So where do you start with communication, and how do you improve your communication style, skills, and abilities?

First you need to learn that we all communicate in our own unique style. We're different. Take some time and find a personality test that shows you the strengths and challenges of the different styles and the varied ways people communicate. Then take the test and uncover your own style. It will be eye-opening. You will learn why and how you gravitate to some people and why you are so confused or repelled by others. When you understand the different ways people communicate, you can see why communication with some is natural and easy, while with others it is quite a challenge.

Next, delve into your personality style to really understand how you communicate. Why do you communicate like you do? There are a number of communication tests or profiles available to help you determine your personality style. I use the

DISC assessment because it is easy to understand and rooted in personal responsiblity. I love personal responsibility. As long as you are open to learning, and you are willing to accept and use the information, any test is valuable.

Then, use this information to learn to really understand other styles. People have varying communication styles and different ways of seeing the world. It is important for you to understand all the styles. You can communicate and connect more effectively when you understand others' motivators, strengths, limitations, and values. When you understand your own style, you are better positioned to learn about the communication styles of people around you. Find out what their strengths, limitations, irritants, and values are.

Lastly, learn to adjust your style to communicate better with others. You are not stuck with the personality style with which you were born. By learning about other personality styles and what they value, you can actually adjust your style to facilitate effective communication with others. Adjusting our style to better connect with someone else's style is like learning to speak their language. They both appreciate and trust it.

For example, let's say you are an energetic, fast-paced, and strong-willed salesperson who makes quick decisions. You are setting up a sales call. If you take a few moments to look for clues, you can get a fair assessment of your prospect's style preferences. For this example, let's say your prospect has lower energy, is slower-paced, and needs time, information, and a relationship before they make a decision. If you know this information at the beginning, you can make a few adjustments to your calling style: speak slower, spend more time developing a relationship to make a connection, and provide more information. You may even consider breaking the decision-making process into a series of smaller decisions so that it is not as overwhelming.

Communication is a powerful tool in the sales process. If you want to turn your prospects into customers, then invest in learning about communication styles and how to adjust yours to facilitate better connections with others.

22 | Solve the Right Problems

Think about how interesting it is to work in sales. You make money by asking people all types of interesting questions, listening to and learning from their answers. How great is that?

Some people miss the fascination of this experience because they enter each call as a salesperson instead of as a problem solver. They enter the call thinking about what they can sell instead of learning about challenges and opportunities facing a prospect and finding ways to help. It is important to remember that your prospects will not be interested unless you can help identify and solve their problems.

Yes, you are a salesperson, but you also play the role of problem-solver. I like to think of sales calls as a break for the business owner: this is his time to sit down and tell you all about his business. He gets to talk about strengths and challenges, the opportunities he sees, and what really keeps him up at night. Because business owners and professionals are so busy, I believe they rarely have this opportunity. A great salesperson provides this opportunity for them. If you want to turn your prospects into customers, then you need to approach each sales call with the mindset of a problem-solver.

For example, when my cable company called, asking me to upgrade my service and add new channels, I listened nicely to the salesman's pitch (which, I will venture to say, most prospects don't do), and then I nicely informed him that we didn't watch much television. However, while he was on the phone, I told him I would like to discuss bundling our services to save money. He immediately tried to talk with me about the new "incredible" channels that his company was offering.

You can guess how the call continued. He tried to sell me a product I did not want; I tried to get him to talk about the service I did want. Yes, I did end the call with my overall cost reduced, but I also knew at the end of the conversation I would never do additional business with that company. I felt this salesperson did not listen, did not care, and had not offered me what I wanted. The sad part is that, as a sales trainer, I know this is not true; it is especially not true that he had nothing of value to offer me. If he had listened, he would have uncovered other ways that his products or services could benefit me. As a result, I would have been ready to listen because he had met my immediate need.

Great problem-solvers have these traits in common:

- They ask great questions.
- They listen.
- They identify the problem.
- They discuss details with the prospect to ensure that they fully understand.
- They make sure the prospect agrees that this is the right problem.
- They create multiple solutions, ensuring that the prospect remains in control.
- They work with the prospect to make the best decision for them.

If you want to turn your prospects into customers, then approach each call with the mindset that you want to help people solve their problems, not yours. Becoming a problem-solver will lead to increased sales for you and your business.

23

Know Your Competition

How can you possibly turn prospects into customers if you do not know your competition? Understanding and gaining intimate knowledge of your competition is an important step to sales success. If you know your competition, you are in a better position to share the strengths, benefits, and overall value of your product or service with your prospect.

Before you can know your competition you first have to discover who they are, what they sell, and why your customer is buying their product or service and not yours. The most effective way to do this is to examine your lost sales. Often when I ask my clients who their competition is, they list four or five company names. However, when we analyze the data, those companies are not the companies to which they are losing the most business.

You don't define your competition; the market and the prospect define your competition. Your prospects determine your competition by deciding who provides more value than you and your company. Often, your competition may not be who you had thought, so don't try to figure it out by looking at which businesses in your area are doing well. Research your lost sales, and determine who gained business from prospects that you want as customers. You may be surprised to learn who your competition is: a peer, a different industry, or perhaps even your prospect's unwillingness to make a decision.

Next you have to know your competitors' strengths and weaknesses. This calls for a competitor analysis. You can have this professionally done, or you can get your family and friends to visit your competition in person, on the phone, or online. Find out their sales pitch, their value points, and what (if any) weaknesses they have. This is an opportunity to meet your competition's sales staff, understand how they engage their prospects, learn about their follow-up process, and discover the price, features, and overall quality of their product.

Lastly, you want to define how you stack up. How are you and your competition similar? What opportunities set your business apart from your competition, and where and why do they surpass you? Then start filling in the gaps. Use this information to redefine your sales pitch to emphasize your strengths, and redefine similarities as minimal expectations. Then work with your team to turn your competitor's weaknesses into opportunities.

I was working with a small hotel chain in Florida that defined their competition as the Hilton, the Marriott, and other hotel chains of that size. We performed a competitor analysis by talking with several past customers who had regularly returned to Florida but had not returned to this hotel chain. Through our analysis we discovered that this chain was not losing business to the Hilton, Marriott, and other large hotels; they were losing it to small, family-owned motels and bed and breakfasts. We also found people chose these competitors over my client because of the atmosphere. All of the facilities were about the same price, equally convenient, and offered comparable amenities; however, the smaller motels and bed and breakfasts emphasized service. They offered homemade cookies and milk at bedtime, a cocktail hour for business travelers, and live wake-up calls, rather than a buzzer or recording. By understanding this, we were able to change the marketing and service delivery for this hotel chain and reposition their strengths to compete better in the market.

When you understand who your true competition is, why your prospects choose them, and what strengths you need to emphasize to compete, you will know how to position your product or service to outshine the competition. Then you can easily turn your prospects into customers.

24 Develop a Passionate Attitude

In the real estate world, they say that the three most important things are location, location, location. In sales, it is attitude, attitude, attitude! If you love what you do, love your product or service, and love sharing it with others, then turning your prospects into customers is not only easy—it is fun!

When I begin to train, coach or develop strategy with a sales team, the first thing that I gauge is the sales leader's attitude and level of enthusiasm. If the leader is not passionate, excited, or motivated about their product and selling in general, then how can I expect the sales team and prospects to be excited? **Attitude is always the place to start.** With the right attitude, the rest will fall into place.

To sell, you have to engage; to engage, you have to communicate; and to communicate, you have to connect. If you want to close more sales, then you need to connect by building trust. Trust is built through consistent positive interaction with a company or individual. The more often you are upbeat and enthusiastic, the more likely you are to build trust. If you want your prospects to buy from you, then you must convey pride, excitement, and confidence about your product or service.

Attitude is vital to the sales process, and, thankfully, it is controllable. It may be a bigger struggle for some, but ultimately you have a choice about whether you are positive or negative. You control the words you speak and the actions you take.

People buy products or services based on how they feel. Certainly the features, facts and statistics play a role, but a prospect takes action based on an emotional connection with the salesperson and the product. The better your attitude, the more likely your prospect will connect with you, and the more likely they are to take an interest in your product or service.

How do you convey your positive attitude and your faith in the product? Take note of how often you smile. Like attitude, smiling is contagious. Increasing your smile factor will increase your likability and approach-ability—two important elements to turn your prospects into customers.

Analyze your words, body language, and thoughts. It is crucial to ask family and friends for feedback. We are often unaware of the negative or sarcastic undertones our speech and body language convey. Asking others for their observations and opinions, relaxing your ego, and taking their advice will make all the difference. Work on your self-talk by routinely increasing the number of positive messages you tell yourself. We already have enough challenges without adding negative thoughts to the list. Positive self-talk will translate into positive conver-sations, body language, and compliments to your prospects. Thought dictates action, and action dictates outcome. It all starts with what is going on inside your head. The right adjustments can go a long way to deliver the right attitude.

Additionally, if you want a positive attitude, you need to surround yourself with positive people. For many of us, the need to feel sorry for or commiserate with others is a constant distraction—a distraction you cannot afford if you want to be good at sales. My favorite quote is, "you are the average of the five people with which you spend the most time." If you want to be positive and upbeat, to convey energy and enthusi-asm, then don't hang out with negative people. If the individuals that you spend time with are positive, upbeat, and energetic, then you cannot help but be that way, too!

25 | Open the Door to Opportunity

If you have been in sales for awhile, you are already familiar with terms like "up sell" or "cross sell," which mean to sell deeper and wider to your customer base. About ten years ago, sales terms like "relationship sales" and "partnering" with your customers came into fashion, as well. Everyone was going to classes and seminars to learn how to convince customers they were different from other salespeople. Unfortunately, most of those courses only taught techniques to make product-pushing a little less obvious.

If you want to turn your prospects into customers, you do need to learn to sell deep and wide, and you also need to learn to develop and build relationships. Why? The last thing you want is for your competitor to offer your customer a valuable product or service simply because you never offered it. That is not only embarrassing; it can be fatal!

Your job as a "relationship" salesperson is to care for your customers. You should understand their business and goals, and then identify multiple ways your product or service could add value. Remember, your prospects understand their business, and they understand their challenges; they are looking to you or other salespeople to provide them with options and solutions.

This is where the "up sell" comes in. I don't like that term, and I don't like its underlying meaning. Instead, I describe this process as selling opportunities and possibilities, giving our prospects choice, power, and control. By providing the prospect with one or more options, you can open his eyes to possibilities and choices that he did not even know existed.

For example, one of my favorite clients owns a large plumbing company. His business is divided evenly between new construction and service. In reviewing his sales process and looking for opportunities to grow his business, we noticed the majority of his new construction work never evolved into service contracts. To take advantage of this opportunity for growth, we simply adjusted his sales proposals and revamped the sales team's conversations to offer two options. The first option was new construction, and the second option was new construction with a one-year service contract with an option to renew. His sales increased, and the process was far more efficient. The salesmen loved it because it was so easy. Ultimately, the prospect had the choice, but more often than not, they chose option two.

If you want to sell possibilities and opportunities, then you must follow these principles:

- **Build trust first.** Do this by not trying to sell more until you have solved the prospect's immediate need.

- **Give the prospect the choice.** Always have more than one option so they feel in control.

- **Explain the benefit of the higher option.** Be sure you can clearly articulate and explain the value of this higher option.

- **Personalize the option.** Listen to the customer and offer products and services that fit their unique needs. Be open to adjusting your offer to better suit a challenge or opportunity your customer has.

- **Don't push.** If they don't choose the higher option, it's okay. Allow the customer to do what is right for them. If you push, you may slam the door on future opportunity.

Turning your prospects into customers is fun when you learn to sell by helping your customers uncover new possibilities and opportunities.

26

Stop Making Cold Calls

If you want to turn your prospects into clients, then stop making cold calls. Do you love calling people you don't know to push your product or service on them? If not, then stop. You know you want to stop, and I'll be the first to tell you your prospects want you to stop. There is a better way.

One Friday afternoon I received a message from a nice man named George in Washington, D.C. He asked me to return his phone call, saying that he had received my name from Vicki "Someone" and she recommended that we talk. Well, I could not recall a Vicki Someone, but since I strive to return all of my phone calls, I called him back. This time I got his voicemail, so I left a nice message explaining that though I did not know Vicki, I hoped he would call me back and let me know who Vicki is and why he was calling. I would be happy to talk. The next time the phone rang, I recognized his number, so I didn't answer. I wanted to see if he would give the reason for his call. Sure enough, he left a nice message with no reason for why he was calling, so naturally I did not return the call. He confirmed my suspicions: this was a cold call!

Monday rolled around, and I was busy running from one meeting to another. When the phone rang, I answered it without looking. George was calling me again. I said hello and listened as he explained again that Vicki "Someone" suggested he call. I interrupted and told him that I do not know Vicki, and I asked why he was calling. He then said that Vicki was a researcher—meaning that she pulls together calling lists for him—and he sells technology for delivering courses online. He asked if I would like to hear more about his online technology or if I was interested in purchasing it. I said no. He pushed a little harder and began explaining his product. Again, I interrupted him, told him that I was not interested, and said thank you as I hung up.

This process could not possibly be enjoyable for George. He made long-distance phone calls just to connect with me. He lost credibility with me on several fronts:

1. He described Vicki as someone who knew me (not true);

2. He would not leave me a message about why he was calling (making me suspicious); and

3. He talked only about himself, his products, and services.

He never asked what I did or inquired about my challenges and opportunities. We never discussed how his product or service would benefit me. We simply discussed his product, his need, and his goals.

He put in considerable effort and gained no return. Calling must have been stressful for him because he told a white lie, and he knew that I was resistant because I kept asking why he was calling. Also, his efforts were ineffective: I did not buy the product and because of his dishonesty, I never plan to buy.

If you want to turn your prospects into customers, then try a different way. Take the time to clearly identify who can benefit from your product or service and invest in building relationships. Your process should involve asking great questions, learning about your prospect, and then finding unique ways that your product or service can add value. Selling should be enjoyable, something that both you and the prospect look forward to. Stop cold calling. Start building relationships. Then all you have to do is sit back and watch your prospects turn into customers!

27 Structure a Series of Small Calls

A sale is nothing more than a series of small sales calls linked together. Often a seller expects to close a sale on the second or third try. Instead, you need to be patient and structure the sales call as a series of small wins rather than one gigantic victory. **Consistent, small, and steady wins add up to a portfolio of solid, repeat customers.**

Let's walk through an example. I received a referral for a prospect who owns a large software company. In part of my research, I discovered he was quite successful, had built the company from scratch, and now his goal was to take his company to another level. He was interested in growth, but he lacked systems and processes to make that happen. He was looking to expand both his personal and professional profile and that of his company in the local market. He also loved music, enjoyed playing guitar, and singing with fellow musicians.

My objectives on this call were to get further acquainted with this man and his company, and to learn what he was looking for, specifically in terms of growth for his company, marketing, strategic planning, and systems/processes. Lastly, I wanted to make sure I secured a date for a follow-up meeting so I could present ideas on how my services could benefit his company.

The questions I asked directly related to my objectives. What was going on in his industry right now? With the economy changing, what was the impact on him and on his company? What did he see as opportunities? What specific challenges kept him up at night? Where did he see the company in the next five years? What did the growth process look like to him? Did he feel his team was ready for change and growth? If he could only focus on two things over the next year, what would those be and why?

The conversation was fascinating. I learned so much just from asking questions and listening intently. When we finished this portion of our initial meeting, I asked him what questions he had for me, which opened up the perfect opportunity to offer a support statement. Prospects usually ask how you think that you can help them, as this prospect did. I suggested that my background in systems thinking, strategic planning, sales, networking, and business coaching provided the skills he was looking for to take his company to the next level. I could help him position his company for solid growth over the next five years. My experience could help him focus his ideas and goals in the form of a strategic plan, and then develop the necessary systems and processes to support it.

I suggested that we set another date within the next week to sit down and discuss the step-by-step process of how this works, with enough time for me to answer any more questions he had and provide any additional information. He accepted immediately. As we finished the meeting, I also recommended three people in the community that he should talk with about expanding his local business, and I offered to make the introductions. Of the three that I recommended, I told my prospect that one was a musician and that they would have some things in common.

It took three formal meetings and a lot of written correspondence to close the deal. It was a great job and a terrific experience lasting more than a year because each sales call led to more ideas and opportunities. I structured the sales-calling process as a series of small wins and turned a prospect into a solid, loyal customer.

Part III
The Follow-Up

Once you have completed the sales call, it's time to plan your follow-up strategy.

If your prospect has decided to become a customer, you'll want to ensure his satisfaction, acquire referrals, increase your offerings, and continue your discussions.

For a great follow-up strategy, you'll need a great sales funnel, a visual aid that is exactly what it sounds like, a funnel illustrating the sales strategy. You'll learn to process your prospects through the funnel, turning them into customers and guiding them into your vessel of profit and accomplishment. Then you can pour them right back into the top, taking them through again, ensuring an even deeper, mutually beneficial, and long-lasting relationship.

Once you have gathered your data, you'll use that information to polish future deliveries and improve your personal confidence level. It's important to keep learning and keep practicing. Even if you are already an accomplished salesperson, this is an important step. Successful businesses change as they grow, products evolve, industries change, and the newcomers to your industry are up-to-speed on the latest news.

42 Rules to Turn Your Prospects into Customers

- Rule 28: Be Patiently Persistent
- Rule 29: Be Visible
- Rule 30: Make It Easy
- Rule 31: Learn to Love Accountability
- Rule 32: Sell to Your Existing Clients
- Rule 33: Work Your Sales Funnel
- Rule 34: Believe That You're an Expert
- Rule 35: Get Back on the Horse
- Rule 36: Learn to Embrace the Power of Focus
- Rule 37: Focus on Goals
- Rule 38: Know When to Walk Away
- Rule 39: Invest in Yourself
- Rule 40: Take the Leap
- Rule 41: Have Fun!
- Rule 42: These Are My Rules. What Are Yours?

28 Be Patiently Persistent

So here you are. You have made the sales call, delivered your best pitch, and you feel sure the next step is simply to close the deal. But unfortunately, nothing happens. You call the prospect and follow up. They say they are interested, yet there is still no movement, and there is still no close to your sale. You feel rejected, you don't understand why, and you're frustrated because the deal did not close. So what do you do? First, understand this is not about you. The prospect is not doing anything to you; they are doing what is best for them. People, even when they are interested or need your product or service, buy when they are ready, not when you are. Certainly you can influence that, but a good salesperson knows not to push it. Present a high quality sales strategy, keep in touch, and let the prospect ultimately decide the timing of the sale.

In sales, patience is a virtue, and stamina is vital! Prospects buy when they are ready, and they buy when your product or service becomes their priority. In this fast-paced world, prospects may be interested in something that you are selling, and they may realize that they need what you are selling; however, your timing to sell and theirs to buy may not coincide perfectly.

You have to understand your product or service does not solve your prospect's most pressing concern. Put your "buyer's cap" on, and you can easily relate to this. Think about it: if your schedule had fewer priorities, there are a number of things you would buy right now.

For example, these things are on my list: I want a new cell phone carrier, I want to update my homeowner's insurance, and I need new tires on my car. I want and need all of these things, but they are not my most pressing concerns each day. However, if a skilled and authentic salesperson targets me, invests in building a relationship, and follows up in a way that steadily increases the value, I would prioritize the sale. As a salesperson, your job is to make the process so easy and so valuable that the prospect's desire to buy increases. Following up in a non-aggressive, but persistent way makes it easy for your buyer to keep in contact. Stay in touch, stay connected, and be visible so that when your prospects are ready, you're the one they come to.

This sales cycle is completely normal and natural. If you recognize that, you will have the edge over your competitors. Salespeople, when put on hold by a prospect, usually do one of two things:

1. They give up; or

2. They get overly aggressive.

Either way, the sale is lost. So how should you handle this?

Last summer, I attended the National Speakers Association Annual Conference and heard one of the best sales professionals speak on this topic. His name is Ed Robinson (see http://www.edspeaks.com). I learned from Ed that in our current economic environment, the number of contacts it takes to turn a prospect into a customer has significantly increased. Now people want to be assured of value. They want to build trust, and they want the time to make decisions. Thus, the sales cycle lengthens.

So how do you stay in touch without becoming annoying? I left Ed's lecture motivated to develop a list of ideas and ways to stay in touch, in front of, and connected to clients without being a pest. As we continue through Part III: The Follow Up, we'll review some of those ideas to continue strengthening your chances to build and grow a successful sales campaign by turning your list of prospects into loyal customers.

29

Be Visible

Visibility and easy access are essential if you want to turn your prospects into customers. You have to be at the top of your prospect's mind when they are ready to buy.

It is not the quantity of interactions that matters; what matters is your consistent approach to quality contacts, high visibility, and easy access. When I discuss the need for consistency with my sales clients, either they want to be more aggressive and "help" their prospect make the decision a little faster, or they fear that any consistent approach will make them annoying to the prospect.

If you try to force your prospect to make the decision, you stand a good chance of losing the sale. If you do land the sale, even with an aggressive approach, you've weakened your chances of future sales. Prospects need to enjoy the sales experience, and forcing them to make a decision does not feel good. On the other hand, not staying in touch consistently pretty much ensures that your competitor will get the sale. Nevertheless, fear of being a bother or annoying to a prospect is completely understandable and is exactly why you need to create a well-thought-out plan.

While your strategy needs to be your own, let's discuss how to get started.

- Start with a brain dump. Get one or two friends to sit down with you and brainstorm ways that you could keep yourself visible with clients.

- Review the list, and check off the ideas that add value or benefit for the prospect.

- Ask one or two of your top customers what things you do (outside of providing your product or service) that add value to them.

- Add those to your list.

- Review the list, and choose the fifteen or twenty ideas with which you feel most comfortable. Your comfort level with a follow-up strategy is key. You are more likely to do something consistently if you enjoy it and look forward to it. Choosing strategies and techniques that put you far outside your comfort zone pretty much guarantees you won't follow through.

- Create your "high-visibility/high-touch" strategy. Put your time and energy into creating this, and you will see your prospects turn into clients much more easily than you ever thought possible.

Here is a strategy checklist to get you started:

- Attend a networking event where you know this prospect will be. Say hello and talk, but do not discuss business.

- Introduce them to another business person that would be a good connection for them.

- Invite them to an event your company is hosting.

- Comment on their status via LinkedIn or Facebook, or retweet them on Twitter.

- Send an article or book regarding a particular business challenge they are having (high-quality, used books are available for under $10 on Amazon).

- Refer business to them, then call them and let them know.

- Invite them to a networking event they may not know about.

- When the time is right, set up another sales call.

You get the idea. Find casual ways to add value, stay visible, and facilitate doing business. For prospects that take longer to close, finding the right balance of visibility, high touch, and actually asking for business is vital. It is different for every prospect, so develop your strategy and listen to your gut. Trust yourself; you'll know when to tread softly, and you'll know when to turn up the heat. The key to turning your prospects into customers is having a strategy for indivudalized follow up.

30
Make It Easy

Have you ever asked yourself if you are an easy business partner? The truth is that you don't know the answer to this question until you ask your customers. First, ask them if you are easy to do business with, and why or why not? Then ask them for ideas on how you could improve the buying process, making it easier for them to do business with you.

You work in your business day in and day out. You understand how the process works, what your acronyms stand for, and which department handles which service. But do your customers know? You can invest in the best marketing and have the most highly-trained sales force, but if you're not easy and enjoyable to do business with, then you will consistently struggle to turn your prospects into customers.

Perhaps you've had an experience like this: You want to buy a new computer, so you search online, visit the local computer stores, ask your computer-tech person, and then finally make a purchase. Everyone said this computer was easy to use and easy to set up. So you are ready to get started, and before you know it, you hit a snag.

While I am sure the rest of the story is familiar, I'll continue for argument's sake. You call the company and are put on hold. Then you get cut off. Then you are passed from department to department; and when you finally are connected to someone who can help you, they talk over your head, are condescending, or do not speak your language. You get off the phone, feeling frustrated and mad, and you vow never to do business with this company again. You end up calling your local computer-tech person and paying an outrageous service fee to fix something that was supposed to be handled through free support. This was a big reason you bought the computer in the first place.

Now, in defense of the company, I do not believe that this is their desired outcome. No one wants customers to be mad, upset, or saying things about them. Then why are some companies so hard to do business with? Why don't they make the customer's experience a priority? I think it is because it just does not cross their mind. They are so caught up in getting the job done or delivering the service that they never stop to think about the customer.

How do you make sure that you are an easy business partner? I have read and researched many complicated ways of doing this, but I think the best method is asking your customer. You can complete the assessment informally or with a formal survey. Several clients have asked me to perform a customer assessment to determine possible improvements that would enhance the customer experience. This process reveals great perspective and additional information, and it is fun.

Another idea is to set up an email marketing system that allows you to contact your customers directly, providing them with coupons or bonuses for assisting you with a survey assessment. People are busy and may not want to find time to fill out a survey. So provide an incentive by giving them something for sharing their valuable opinion with you.

Making sure that you are easy to do business with makes prospects happy about their decisions, makes customers loyal, and makes advocates happy to keep sending business your way! If you want to turn your prospects into customers, make sure your customers believe you are easy to do business with.

Learn to Love Accountability

I love accountability! It is one of the most important themes in the sales process, but it has received a bad rap over the years. I would like to be among the first to say that if you want to turn your prospects into customers, then you need to learn to love accountability.

For most salespeople, the term accountability brings up painful images of a stern sales manager who hounds you daily, continuously asking how many sales calls you made, and how many products you sold. What did you close; who are you calling on, and how much money did you make? That kind of accountability is exhausting. No wonder people hate the word.

Accountability is really about practice, consistency, and learning. If you want to be good at anything, you have to practice consistently and learn from your accomplishments and your mistakes. You can only do that if you set up a method of accountability. Accountability is the story of "you."

If you want to turn your prospects into customers, then you must track your behaviors, measure your progress, and learn from your results. There is true gold in that information. Process and consistency are critical to great sales results, but if you do not take the time to learn from what you are doing, then how can you ever hope to improve?

One of my favorite stories about accountability actually comes from a friend of mine, Myra Holbert. She is a conference sales manager in Texas. She has a staff of about twenty-five salespeople working directly for her. A few years ago, she had her newest members of the sales team call existing clients, trying to drum up new business. Being a great sales manager, she had each person track his or her calls and results. Each Friday they had a quick sales meeting to review calls made and services sold. At this time, she noticed that her newest salesperson was enthusiastically making plenty of calls, but seeing very little in the way of results.

Myra asked to speak with her after the meeting. She brought her into the office, and asked her to talk about her sales experience. She made sure to compliment her on the high number of sales calls she made, and then asked her what challenges she faced with closing deals. The salesperson said that while she called and called, the customers showed very little interest in doing any additional business. Myra smiled and told her not to worry. As a salesperson, she was doing the hardest part by making the calls. Myra guessed that by adjusting just a sentence or two in her approach, the results would be far different. Myra offered to make calls with her that afternoon, giving her the opportunity to listen to Myra talk with customers. To make a long story short, they spent the afternoon working together, adjusting delivery, and improving sales style. The results were a significant increase in the number of closed leads and a highly-motivated new salesperson.

This could not have happened if Myra did not hold her team accountable. I love accountability because it is how you learn. If you track what you are doing and you don't get the desired result, then it may not be from a lack of effort. It may be from your technique, your skill, or perhaps choosing the wrong prospects.

Schedule time to review your progress. You can learn what you do well, work to improve what you don't do well, and turn far more prospects into customers!

32

Sell to Your Existing Clients

The easiest people to sell to already buy from you. The best prospects are your existing clients, and the only reason they are not buying more is because you are not offering more. **If you want to make selling easy and more rewarding, then sell deeper and wider to your existing customers.** Most salespeople sell one product or service to a prospect, and then they move on to the next. This leaves the total needs of the prospect unmet, and the door wide open for your competitors to come in and steal the relationship.

Make a list of all the products and services that you offer. Then make a list of your top thirty customers. Match the products or services that they need to the number that they buy from you. I'm betting that the needs of your customers far outweigh the number of products and services that they buy from you. The good news is it's not too late to change this ratio. You have just created a great prospect list, one that is going to be an easy sell.

For starters, these "prospects" already know your company and consider themselves to be customers. They already know you and would welcome a call from you. Plus, they have purchased from you in the past, and they most likely trust and value what you tell them. Closing the next deal should be a piece of cake!

Why create a prospect list full of your existing customers?

It is expensive to attract new customers, and there is no guarantee that you will land their business. The cost of attracting new customers can be up to seven or eight times more expensive than selling to an existing client. In addition, by selling more to existing clients, you know that they will remain your customers. The more products and services they buy, the deeper the relationship becomes; and the deeper the relationship, the less likely they are to take their business elsewhere.

Cold calls are difficult. For most salespeople, the most stressful part of the call is the beginning. Getting in the door, establishing the relationship, and making that first sale can be intimidating. With existing clients, that part is over. You already did all the hard work, so why not sit back and reap the rewards? Let your competitors make the cold calls. Let them be stressed and burned out, not you.

Additional sales will build your reputation. As a salesperson, your customers place their trust in you. If you continue to share information with them and offer products and services that benefit their business, this trust and value will grow. You will move from being just their salesperson to being their advocate and trusted advisor.

They will start to call you. The better that you care for your existing customers, the better your reputation will become. Customers will call you. You will have taught them to work with you to fill their needs. You have all the answers. Then they start telling their friends, their neighbors, and perfect strangers to call you.

If you want to turn your prospects into customers, then one-half to one-third of your prospect list should be filled with your existing customers. There is "gold" in these relationships!

33 Work Your Sales Funnel

If you want to turn your prospects into customers, then you have to manage your own sales process. Whether or not you have a sales manager, a boss, or anyone else that may hold you accountable, you will be more successful if you take personal responsibility for achieving your sales goals.

Start by overfilling your sales funnel. What's a sales funnel, you may ask, and why do you have to overfill it? It is exactly what it sounds like: a funnel that illustrates the sales process. This kind of visual representation drives home the importance of systematically performing all parts of the sales process in order to achieve maximum results. You overfill it so you can breathe easy, relax, and allow your prospects to move through the funnel at their own pace.

It is also a great learning device. I go through my sales funnel on a weekly basis to see what went "into" the funnel and what "came out" of it. In other words I assess what steps are going well, where a breakdown may have occurred, what actions are worth repeating, and what simple improvements I can make to produce better results. The sales funnel is a quick, easy and highly effective way to hold yourself accountable.

I call this "The Effective Sales Funnel" because this is my version of how a sales funnel needs to work (see Appendix B). Let's review its levels starting from the top:

Defined Target Market and Established Goals
I always start by asking myself, "How closely did I focus on my target market, and how accountable was I to meeting my established behavior goals? What was the result?" In other words, did I connect with those individuals most likely to do business with me? Did I meet my behavior goals—number of events attended, sales calls made, sales follow-up calls made, etc.?

Targeted Networking
Which events did I attend? Was my target market there? Did I work to meet and connect with my target market? What was the result?

Prospect List
Who did I add to my prospect list from networking events? What was my justification for adding them to my list? What was the result?

Structured Sales Calls
How many sales calls did I go on? Did I follow the structure? What was the result?

Qualified Sales Follow-Up Calls
How many follow-up calls did I make? What was the quality of those calls? Did I set and meet objectives? What was the result?

Goals
Am I meeting my behavior and growth goals? If so, what is working? If not, where (in the funnel) is the problem? What is working well and what can I improve?

Using a sales funnel as part of your weekly accountability is one of the easiest and quickest ways to establish what is working in your sales process and what might be slowing you down. Your sales funnel tells you a story. It quickly and easily shows where you are excelling at your sales process and where exactly you are getting stuck. That is powerful information you can use to make the changes or get the support you need to be more effective.

As we discussed in Rule 31, **if you want to make sales fun and less stressful, then you need to use accountability to learn, make adjustments, and move the sales process forward.** Design your own sales funnel, use it on a weekly basis, and you'll rapidly improve your ability to turn your prospects into customers.

34 Believe That You're an Expert

Prospects need a reason to choose to do business with you. Understand that for them, even in the most positive situations, it is still a hassle and an interruption to move services or change a product they are using. They need a solid and strong reason to change.

You can sell the features and benefits of your products and services all day long, but the prospect will decide to do business with you based ultimately on who you are and what you bring to the table personally. You need to be someone that your prospects and customers can rely on for good information and quality advice—an expert. You need to know more about your industry, your product or service, and your market than anyone else does. You need to be confident in your ability to teach the benefits of your product and service.

I do not mean that you need to publish books, be the subject of magazine articles, or be featured on television shows. I do mean that you have to believe you are an expert, and you have to establish that reputation among your peers, competitors, and your customers.

There was a great article in the Harvard Business Review a few years ago entitled "The Making of an Expert." The article explains how someone is defined or labeled an expert by meeting the following three expectations.

- Performs in a manner that is consistently superior to that of their peers

- Produces concrete results
- Provides replicable and measurable services

The next question, then, is how do you become an expert in your industry?

Study and master your craft.
You need to dedicate yourself continuously to learning about your product or service, and to learning about your industry. You need to read books, listen to CDs, attend conferences, and watch DVDs. You need to know the latest trends, know what valid information is coming out, what works, and what does not. If you want your prospects and your peers to view you as an expert then you need to be able to offer credible ideas, resources, and information. In other words, you need to know what you are talking about!

Practice.
If you want to be good at something, you have to practice. You need to prepare. Spend time role-playing, working in front of the mirror, and even "performing" for the family pet.

Measure and improve.
In your quest to become an expert, measuring your efforts and results becomes even more important. If you want to become an expert and remain one, you need to understand your sales results and be consistently looking for ways to improve them. Measurement helps you remain at your peak performance level.

Promote.
You need to make an effort to promote your reputation as an expert. You need to become the go-to person in your community in your field of expertise. How? You can hold volunteer positions that highlight your expertise, or you can help a number of highly visible pro bono clients each year. Also, just by adding value quickly and up-front with prospects, your reputation as the go-to person will increase. Giving limited advice and insight early on with prospects gives them a taste of what they will receive when they work with you full-time. When you are networking or on a sales call, find out what issues people are dealing with that relate to your product or service, and give them advice, share an article, or make a connection for them. This will position you as the go-to person in your field of expertise.

Becoming an expert takes time, dedication, and focus. But in the end, what you gain in confidence, enhanced reputation, client growth, and loyalty makes it all worth it.

Get Back on the Horse

No one likes rejection. When you really stop and think about it, though, rejection is only the prospect saying that your product or service does not have enough value for them at this time. When you put it that way, "no" is actually good information for you to have. It means you should go back to the planning stage of your calling efforts and think about how you could add more value. "No" does not mean never. "No" means no right now.

If you want to turn your prospects into clients, you must learn to be persistent. You need to accept rejection, learn from it and have enough stamina to get back on the horse and try again. Persistence actually means lasting or enduring tenaciously; if you want to be good at anything, including sales, you have to be persistent.

I think a big concern after hearing "no" is that others will find us annoying. Here is my plan for being persistent without being annoying.

Thank the customer.
Whenever I lose a sale to a competitor, or a prospect says "no," I make sure to thank the prospect for their time, their consideration, and for the information they shared about their company and their needs. I am sincere in my thank-you, which leaves the prospect with a positive feeling about me. Remember, buying is emotional. Leaving your prospect with a positive feeling about you leaves the door open for future sales.

Make sure you heard the customer.
When the customer says "no," sit down and take a few moments to try to understand why. Often you'll learn that you were not solving the right problem or understanding what is going on in their life. Perhaps you offered the wrong solution, or your timing is off, as they have bigger fish to fry right now.

Know your customer.
Go back to the research phase of the sales call and learn more. The amount of information you know about your prospect is vital to understanding where, when, and how to sell to them. If you heard the word "no," you may not know enough about your prospect and, therefore, you don't deserve the business—yet!

Send an eleventh-hour letter.
If you lose business to a competitor, always send an eleventh-hour letter. This is a letter to help ensure that if for any reason the prospect changes their mind, they feel welcome and comfortable coming back to you. Once people reject you, they may feel awkward or embarrassed to call on you if things do not work out with your competitor. Make sure that you do everything to keep that door open. That way, when they are looking for new opportunity or their salesperson is not delivering, you are the first person that they think to call.

Overfill your sales funnel.
Sales take time. By having plenty of prospects to call on and plenty of opportunities to pursue, you keep yourself from being desperate. If you focus on listening, adding value, and being approachable, prospects will become your customers in their own time. You need to have enough prospects in your pipeline that you stay aware of the level of need and pace of each prospect.

Learning to embrace rejection, being persistent, and building your stamina are all key to your ability to turn your prospects into customers. If you fall off that horse, remember to think about what you learned, put these five steps into action, and get right back on to try again.

36 Learn to Embrace the Power of Focus

Focus amazes me. I find the results that true focus produces to be just incredible. Learning to focus is one of the most useful skills for turning your prospects into customers and for achieving your goals in life. Believe me, google the words "easily distracted" and my name will appear. I want to try everything, participate in anything, travel to anywhere, and enjoy it all! I say all this because when I tell you that focus is powerful and that anyone can do it, I come with the credibility to back it up. It took me a long time to embrace the concept of focus and then to train my wide-open personality to do it. I am so glad that I took the time! The ability to focus is a powerful tool in turning your prospects into customers.

Let me share a story with you. When I first started in banking (in the days when a loan actually required cash flow), my role as a business-banking manager was to start up our company's business-banking department and make sure that we achieved our goals. This was challenging, to say the least, because we started from scratch; and while there was great opportunity, there was a lot of competition. We offered so many different products and services, and we knew there was an unlimited number of existing clients and prospects who could benefit. My boss, Jeff Ward, called me into his office and brought up this strange concept of focus. It sounded like a rule to me, so I was naturally resistant. He wanted to focus on just business loans for our product and focus on professionals (doctors, attorneys, CPAs) for our prospects. Were we still going to sell other products and services, and were we still going to work with other prospects outside of professionals? Absolutely! However, our focus, our proactive daily activities, he said, would be directed at this market.

Again, I was resistant, as it sounded limiting to me. He persisted and we set a goal (in other words, a focus) to book $350,000 a month in business loans. We worked with our team to determine our prospect list of professionals and the specific daily actions we were going to take. Our progress was amazing! Within two months, our team was blowing that goal out of the water. Jeff suggested we increase our focus to $1,000,000 a month, so we refined our prospect list and increased the quality of our daily actions. I was a little doubtful that we could do it, but by year's end, we were booking $3,000,000–$4,000,000 a month in business loans consistently, and we banked most of the community's most successful professionals. **The power of focus is incredible!** It is also amazingly simple.

Below are some tips to help you focus:

Your focus needs to be clear. In order to keep your focus clear, you need to define what it is you hope to accomplish.

Your focus can change. Nothing ever stays the same. If it's necessary to adjust your focus to get better results, then do so.

Focus requires hard work. Focus is a simple concept that is not easy. It takes work, discipline, and commitment.

Your focus needs to be persistent. You will make mistakes. You may not always receive the results you hoped for instantly, but your diligence will pay off in time.

Your focus needs to have goals. Setting goals, both short- and long-term, is an important part of the focusing process. You need something worthwhile to focus on and measure.

We will discuss goals more thoroughly in the next rule. You need to use your power of focus to set large and small objectives, which will guide you to your destination of successful sales.

37 Focus on Goals

Now that you've embraced the power of focus, you need to give your mind something on which to focus. These steps will show you how to focus on your goals and improve your ability to accomplish them.

Begin with the understanding of how your company makes money.

That may sound a little unconventional, but for goals to have meaning and purpose, you need to understand why they are your goals. I advise all of my clients to get a good grasp on how they make and how they lose money. When you understand specifically how your business gains and loses profits, you can adjust your goals to ensure your daily actions are producing a positive return on investment.

I also advise my clients to teach their employees how the company makes money. Doing this will open eyes, shift paradigms, and give the knowledge needed to focus on the right things. One of the questions my clients ask me most often is how to motivate their teams and how to get them to take ownership. My answer is: First, ensure your employees understand their purpose, their role, and the value in both. People statistically perform higher and more consistently when they understand why their job is important and how specifically to best contribute.

Set a financial and visual goal.

It is good to have a financial goal and a visual goal, a number that you want to achieve and a visual of how that will look. The number provides the technical focus, and the visual provides the emotional focus. In the example in Rule 36, we set a goal of booking $1,000,000 a month in business loans, and we knew that type of business growth would bring us the President's Award, which it did. The financial and the visual goal made a powerful combination that drove our ability to focus and stay motivated.

Connect behaviors to the goal.
In other words, how specifically are you going to focus? What daily actions are you going to take to meet your goals? For example, how many networking events are you going to attend? How many sales calls are you going to make? How many sales follow-up calls do you plan to make? *Defining your behaviors is simply a way of creating your plan to focus.*

Hold yourself accountable.
There's that word again. Track and measure your daily behaviors, then hold weekly meetings to see how you are doing with achieving your goals. This is essential in your ability to learn which behaviors are producing results, and which ones are hindering results.

A fifteen-, thirty-, or sixty-minute meeting once a week is a great invest-ment of time. Better yet, if you are part of a team, having these meetings as a group can bring incredible insight, peer-to-peer coaching, and improved teamwork.

Commit to improving.
You need to commit to keep doing what is working and improving what is not working. Ask yourself, "Do I need to improve my skills? Do I need to make more calls? Should I choose better prospects? Is it necessary to be better prepared for calls? Can I follow up more? Whatever it is, if you want to reap the benefits of focus, then you need to commit to im-proving.

Laugh, enjoy it, and have fun.
Focusing and achieving your goals is fun! Focus on what you hope to achieve, set long-term and short-term goals, and have fun trying to reach them.

When you and your team use these steps, it's fun to accomplish your goals, and a fat bottom line is inevitable!

38 Know When to Walk Away

The hard truth about sales is that very few prospects are going to tell you "no" directly. Unfortunately, it is human nature. Most of us do not like confrontation, and we don't like telling people "no."

Unfortunately for salespeople, this translates into wasted time, effort, and money spent on prospects who never plan to buy. If you want to turn your prospects into customers, then you have to know when to walk away. In other words, you need to learn to manage your sales efforts so that you focus on those prospects with the highest probability of buying from you.

I work with a large firm in South Carolina, coaching and training the sales team. When I started two years ago, several sales professionals were struggling to close deals. One salesman named John worked on the same client for over a year. John and I sat down to discuss why he felt the prospect wasn't buying and what his options were. When we took the time to analyze the situation, we found John had been pursuing a prospect who had a low probability of ever buying his product. Why was the probability so low? This prospect had been using a competitor's product for years, and his sales representative had been calling on him for more than twenty years. They not only did business together, but they also played golf together regularly. The prospect had also been recognized and rewarded by the competitor company, was given special discounts, and had been featured in testimonial ads.

When John and I stepped back to take in all this information, it was obvious this prospect should not have been at the top of his list. By knowing when to walk away from one prospect, John could have called on four or five others.

While that is a straightforward example, it amazes me that many sales-people never step back to analyze why a prospect is not buying. Instead, they keep trying to convince the prospect, and they wind up frustrated, unmotivated, and burned out.

How do you strike a balance between persistence and knowing when to walk away? You need to establish your sales criteria. These are your guidelines of where, when, and how you determine the likelihood that a prospect will buy.

You should develop your own guidelines, but here are the top ten criteria that I use:

1. Does the prospect understand that they have a need?
2. How is that need currently being met or not met?
3. How solid is my relationship with the prospect?
4. Am I calling on the person who has the power to make a decision?
5. Do I feel my prospect is engaged?
6. How hard is it to get follow-up appointments for second, third, or fourth calls?
7. Does the person seem interested in meeting with me?
8. Does my prospect do his or her part to move the sales process forward (i.e., by providing information, giving me access to people with whom I need to talk, reviewing information I provide, etc.)?
9. How often does this prospect change providers?
10. Are there obstacles in my way that are beyond my control?

Knowing when to walk away does not mean that you will never do business with this prospect or that you should not stay in contact with him. Walking away means your time and energy will be spent wisely by working with other prospects that have a higher probability of buying your product and closing the deal.

Invest in Yourself

When is the last time your name appeared at the top of your to-do list? When is the last time you blocked off even fifteen minutes just to work on personal growth and development? My guess is that it has been awhile. If you want to turn your prospects into customers, the first investment you need to make as a salesperson is in yourself.

Your prospects are relying on you to be confident, to be the expert, to have ideas, and to provide solutions. You have to be at the top of your game if you are going to deliver.

I realize that we are all pressed for time, and I am certainly not advising you to spend days on end reading books, watching videos, or attending seminars. I do advise that you dedicate time each day to improving your skills and talents as a salesperson. Scheduling small amounts of time every day for personal growth and development is manageable, and it has a powerful impact on results. The magic is in the brevity and the consistency.

I am an early riser: I love to get up in the morning, make a pot of coffee, and enjoy the peace, quiet, and alone time of the morning. I invest this time in myself by learning something about business development, business trends, strategic planning, or other topics that help me to be at the top of my game. I read books, a chapter at a time; I read articles, no more than two or three per session. Or, I can usually watch several short videos and still have time to take notes and develop plans on how to implement what I learn. I feel this practice puts me in pretty good company. David Nour, founder and CEO of Atlanta-based Relationship Economics, is one of my favorite experts to follow (see http://www.relationshipeconomics.net). I read his blog, belong to his social network, and soak up as much of his knowledge and expertise as I can. One of the first things I heard him say in a lecture was that he devotes an hour every day to learning. An hour every day! This man is already recognized as being at the top of his game; he is an expert in the field of social networking and relationship technology. He works with Fortune 500 companies worldwide, helping them to design and implement social networks. With all that he has accomplished, he still respects the importance of investing time in himself consistently. I suspect that he knows this time is what keeps him valuable to his clients and ahead of his competition.

Your prospects are paying you for your knowledge, whether you realize it or not. The more value you can add to yourself, as well as to that of your product or service, the more likely you are to close the deal and keep the relationship for the long term. Prospects need you to be an expert on your product or service, as well as the market, your competition, and the latest trends. Now more than ever, prospects need confident salespeople who can help them on multiple levels.

If you want to turn your prospects into customers, then invest in yourself. It takes dedication and commitment to personal growth and development, but it will yield the highest ROI you will ever make!

Take the Leap

No sales coach, no matter how good, is actually going to make your sales calls for you. Your coach can go with you, if you'd like, and support you on the call, but the actual growth of your sales portfolio is up to you and you alone. The most important part of sales—the actual "doing it" part—is something that you need to execute.

While all of the other steps are important, none of them matter if you don't actually make the call. Making the call is important because you begin to build a relationship with your client, you learn how to sell, and you build the bottom line and produce revenue.

So why do we fail to execute? I attribute part of this failure to the "gym membership concept." In other words, some people think that by cutting the check or swiping the credit card, they will instantly reap the benefits of the purchase. Unfortunately, there is no free lunch. If you want to gain the rewards of selling (or going to the gym), then you have to execute. Take if from Nike, "Just do it!"

The reasons why people fail to execute usually fall into one of the following categories:

Fear
You are simply scared to execute. When you break it down, this actually makes sense. Most of us are afraid to try new things. We are naturally resistant to change. When we know this, it makes it easier to accept our fear and understand it is normal. However, we also have to

realize that the only way to get past fear is to do the task, gain experience, and get comfortable with the process. Children jump in with such enthusiasm because they don't waste time convincing themselves they can't or thinking about what might happen. They just do it!

Data Distraction
You research, gather information and study to the point of exhaustion. Remember, we said to be prepared, not overqualified. Selling does not have to be perfect; it just needs to happen. Don't get lost in over-studying or over-planning. Sure, you need to be prepared before you go on calls, but you do not need to be able to pass an exam. Gather your information, and go make the call!

Inept Accountability
If no one is holding you accountable, including yourself, then there is a good chance you are not going to execute. Studies show that people with coaches are eighty percent more likely to produce results than those without. While your boss or your coach is a great person to hold you accountable, personal accountability needs to be at the top of your list if you truly want to be effective. Remember, accountability is about learning. Understand what you are doing well, what you need to improve, and make the necessary changes.

Personal Investment
Effective execution is the result of confidence. You need to learn your skill, invest in your education, and continue to learn from your results. Increase your investment in yourself, and you will increase your ability to execute.

The need to go on the sales call will not go away, no matter how much you avoid it or how many excuses you have. At the end of the day, if you want to turn your prospects into customers, take the leap and make the calls.

41

Have Fun!

We have covered ideas, strategies, and rules on how to sell and sell effectively, but you must remember to relax, enjoy it, and have fun with the process. Turning your prospects into customers depends so much on your sustainability, your desire to do this job long-term.

The best salespeople I know are happy. You can tell they love their jobs, and they love the opportunity to talk with you about how they can help. One that comes to mind is Rusty Owen, a business development officer with JPS. When you see Rusty walking your way, he has a confident swagger and a big grin on his face. You can't help but smile back. He will be the first to tell you that he loves what he does. When you are with him, you feel yourself getting happy, too. Rusty invokes an energy that makes you want to be around him. With that type of effect on people, consider the likelihood that his prospects will turn into customers.

Relax.
Remember, Rome was not built in a day! You do not have to master every aspect of sales strategy right away. You do not have to have the perfect prospect list, and you do not have to have all the answers. Just get started by focusing on what you are good at, and commit to learn what you don't know. No one ever masters sales, no one ever has a perfect year, and no one is ever free of making mistakes. Focus on the positive, and

embrace the negatives as growth opportunities. In other words, you can relax. You are on the road to improvement!

Enjoy.
Even if it does not come naturally to you, put a smile on your face. We enjoy things more when we smile. Plus, it becomes more likely that our prospects will smile. If you think I am kidding, spend today watching people who smile. You will find yourself smiling back much of the time.

Tell yourself every morning that you love what you do, and remind yourself why. Reward yourself for the positive things that happen, no matter how small. Set a goal to reward yourself with positive praise, three to four times a day. This will encourage your mind to prioritize the positive, and keep you enjoying the process.

Have Fun!
Find a reason to laugh during the day. Humor is a great sales tool, and it makes life so much easier. Seek out people who make you laugh, look for the humor in stressful situations, and help others have fun in the workplace. Especially in these changing economic times, people need reasons to have fun. When you decide to bring humor into the workplace, you help everyone.

I am on a mission; I want you to learn to love sales! I want you to understand that sales can and should be fun, rewarding, and something to be passionate about. I started out hating sales, but came to realize that I had learned habits and behaviors that took the fun out of the process. If you find yourself hating sales, then find a strategy or a coach that can help you learn to love it. If you want to turn your prospects into customers, then you need to relax, enjoy, and have fun!

42

These Are My Rules. What Are Yours?

This book began by discussing the fact that sales is far more of an art than a science, and that each situation is different. Selling is just not black and white. It takes skill, knowledge, and flexibility to adjust to each situation in order to be truly successful. Continuous learning plays a large role in your sales success.

We have covered a vast array of rules for how to turn your prospects into customers. Now, I'd like to hear from you. What rules do you use that have proven valuable to your success? What are your rules for successful sales, and which ones specifically help you turn your prospects into customers?

My clients, audiences, and friends share their rules with me all the time. They know I love to hear them, and I love to add them to my list. A few years ago, I was speaking at a convention in Orlando and came to my favorite part of the presentation. I asked the audience about their rules for successful sales. A member of the audience jumped up and was anxious to share her rule.

She started by saying that time had always been a factor for her as a salesperson. She had taken countless time-management courses and seminars, picking up some good tactics and ideas, but they still did not solve her problem. She ultimately found an answer that became her new rule: "Manage your priorities, not your time!" In other words, understand that we can all control where we focus our energy; own that control and implement a strategy that makes your energy work for you. She cautioned us all to remember that we are in charge, and we have choices in what we do or don't do in a given day. Change came for her when she realized everyone else was controlling her time, and she was the only person who had no say in what her day, week, or even month looked like. Right then and there, she took charge of her time, decided how she wanted to spend it and with whom. She established her priorities. In doing so, she became more successful, effective, and happy when she learned to mange her priorities and focused her energy on positive and productive behaviors.

Learn to love sales by being open to learning to love not only the process, but the art of implementation. This is where learning from, watching, and sharing with others can truly pay off. Delivery, style, subtle shifts of words and motions can make all the difference in how well you connect with a prospect. When you commit yourself to continuous learning with sales, when you commit to share your talents and skills with others, you will find that you are following the same rules, but your confirmed appointment numbers increase, your sales close faster, and your bottom line starts to move in a positive direction. Share your ideas, your rules, and your strategies for success, and together we can all achieve a more positive and productive sales experience.

A Bonus Rules

Implement the Five C's of Selling.

Learning new sales techniques is important, but these methods cannot determine if you embody the basics. The basics are the fundamentals, the ground rules that determine whether selling is a good career choice for you.

I call these ground rules the "Five C's of Selling." I use the Five C's of Selling to help companies choose and develop good salespeople and sales leaders, and to help small business owners and entrepreneurs determine if they should enlist others to help them sell their services. If you read these Five C's of Selling and find that you may be lacking in any of these areas, then commit to develop these skills. You need all five in place, working together, if you want to make turning prospects into customers a fun, easy, and effective process. So let's see how you stack up!

Care about People.

You have to ask yourself if you genuinely care about and are interested in people. Learning about people in detail is a large part of sales: you have to want to listen to their stories, learn about their companies, and empathize as they share their challenges and opportunities. This is how you gain insight on how you can help and in what ways your product or service can support this prospect. Without genuine care and interest, your ability to uncover opportunity and gain new business will be lacking.

Be *Consistent* in Your Sales Behaviors and Actions.

You have to develop and implement a sales process, a consistent set of actions and behaviors that you use every day. This does not have to be a large number; consistent action is far more important than volume. Consistency will breed improvements in quality and results. Prospects buy when they are ready, not necessarily when you are ready to sell. With a well-organized routine, you will be top-of-mind and ready to respond when prospects are ready to take action.

Enhance Your Ability to *Connect* and Relate.

You need to be able to relate to people and move them to action. Self-awareness is key here; improve your self-awareness, and you will improve your ability to communicate. The better you know yourself, your strengths, your weaknesses, and your communication style, the more ability you'll have to understand and communicate with others. Truly understanding your communication style, as well as the styles of others, enables you to adjust your style and better relate, making prospects feel understood and heard.

Develop Your Sales *Competency*.

Knowledge, expertise, and the desire to continue to grow and develop are essential traits if you want to master sales. The top salesmen are experts in their field, both at the art of selling, and as it relates to their industry, product or service. If you want to enjoy selling, if you want to truly help your prospects and customers, then you need to commit to continual personal development and ongoing growth in your sales process and your industry.

Affirm and Act on Your *Commitment*.

You must ask yourself about your desire and drive. Do you really want to be an accomplished salesperson? Do you want to spend time learning about other people, their businesses, and ways that you can help them grow and succeed? Are you willing to work a sales process and commit to the daily actions and behaviors that are necessary? Are you willing to develop your communication skills and improve your ability to relate to others? Are you willing to learn from rejection, to be open to constantly learning new strategies and methods, and to work when the prospect or client needs you, not according to your schedule? Whatever you choose to do in life, your commitment is the key to your success.

If you embody the basics, the Five C's of Selling, then the answer to turning your prospects into customers is simply a matter of learning and following the rules.

Seal the Deal

I believe turning your prospects into customers largely depends on your effective delivery of the triple threat strategy—position, market, sell! While sales is important, your prospects are more likely to turn into customers if you position and market yourself at the same time you're implementing your powerful sales strategy.

So what does that mean—position, market, sell? **Position** means the image you have in the community—your reputation, your brand, if you will. **Market** means your strategies for consistently making people aware of specficially what you do and the value you offer. **Sell** means actually making calls and asking for the business. Sales is so much easier if before you ever approach your prospects, they have actually heard of you, have a positive image of you, and understand the value that your product or service offers. You can create that positive image and awareness through positioning and marketing.

To discover your position, start by asking yourself a few questions:

- What value and benefit can my product provide?
- Why should prospects or customers care about the value and benefit of my product?
- What is unique or different about my product or service from my competitors'?

For example, in my business, the value that my customers receive is the skill to increasingly convert their prospects into customers. They care because their revenues increase, and they are now confident in executing the necessary skills to generate additional business. Finally, I am unique because I teach people to sell according to their style so the process feels comfortable, is unique to them, and is actually fun, easy, and effective.

Once you establish your position, you need to market it. Again, for professional marketers this is a broad term: marketing is complex. For specifics on how to market, it is best to talk with a professional; but in an attempt to keep it simple, marketing means getting the word out. Once you have established your position in the marketplace, how will you consistently spread your message so that potential customers can learn about you, the value you add, and the benefit that you can bring to their company? There are a variety of ways that you can market yourself—you can write articles, advertise, use social media, public speaking, seminars, etc.

If you want to make the sales process easier and more effective, you need to position, market, and sell. Prospects need to have heard of you, understand clearly what you sell, and connect to the value you offer long before you ever show up at their door.

If you position yourself and market yourself, it becomes so much easier to make the sales call, establish a relationship with the prospect, and close the deal. You cannot expect positioning and marketing to lead to closed deals without working your sales process properly. Conversely, you cannot expect to have a high closing ratio of deals without positioning and marketing yourself. You have to do all three.

Positioning, marketing, and sales are a powerful combination, and the style of delivery is unique to each salesperson. It doesn't matter how you do it, just that you do it. If you want to turn more prospects into customers, then position, market, and sell!

B | Sales Funnel

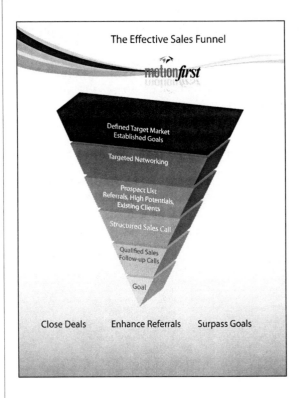

The Effective Sales Funnel

motion*first*

Defined Target Market
Established Goals

Targeted Networking

Prospect List
Referrals, High Potentials,
Existing Clients

Structured Sales Call

Qualified Sales
Follow-up Calls

Goal

Close Deals   Enhance Referrals   Surpass Goals

Appendix

C Resources

Blogs/Websites

http://www.relationshipeconomics.com

http://www.edspeaks.com

http://www.sethgodin.typepad.com

http://www.edbrenegar.typepad.com

http://www.about.com

http://www.allbusiness.com

http://www.personalityinsights.com

Books

How to Win Friends and Influence People—Dale Carnegie

The Confidence Plan—Tim Ursiny, PhD

The Brand Gap—Marty Neumier

Dig Your Well before You're Thirsty—Harvy Mackay

Never Eat Alone—Keith Ferrazzi

Purple Cow—Seth Godin

Relationship Economics—David Nour

The Million Dollar Rainmaker—Rainmaker Strategies for Business Growth—Ed Robinson

About the Author

Meridith Elliott Powell, founder and owner of MotionFirst, will catalyze and inspire your leadership and sales team.

After an award-winning career in marketing, sales, and finance, Meridith left corporate America to strike out on her own. Today, as founder of MotionFirst, Meridith works with professionals and companies to help them turn "busy" into "productive" by enhancing their networking, sales, and service skills.

As a certified strategist, coach, and business development expert, Meridith has the skills and the knowledge to bring your "numbers" side and your "people" side together, to align your company's goals, and escalate your profitability.

Meridith's signature style and her ability to rapidly connect with individuals make her a sought-after speaker, trainer, and coach.

Meridith is passionate about helping clients develop strategies, business development plans, and leadership programs that will engage their teams and drive the bottom line. She has the ability to break down complex issues to make them easy to understand and easy to implement.

Meridith is among a handful of strategists who hold the gold master-certification in Strategic Planning conferred by the University of San Diego. A master-certified Human Behavior Specialist, Meridith's certification confirms her talents as an instructor, coach, and specialist in communication styles, human behaviors, and their impact on professional relationships and organizational development.

What does this mean to you? That Meridith can give you a map to success and the keys to unlock hidden talents for selling and planning within your employees and within yourself.

Meridith also has second-level certification in Emotional Intelligence (EQ). Her powerful combination of business coaching and EQ certification gives her an amazing ability to support her clients in their efforts to master the technical and relationship-building skills needed to be successful in today's competitive environment.

Meridith serves a wide range of clients, including financial and legal firms, construction firms, and a wide variety of health care providers.

Write Your Own Rules

You can write your own 42 Rules book, and we can help you do it—from initial concept, to writing and editing, to publishing and marketing. If you have a great idea for a 42 Rules book, then we want to hear from you.

As you know, the books in the 42 Rules series are practical guidebooks that focus on a single topic. The books are written in an easy-to-read format that condenses the fundamental elements of the topic into 42 Rules. They use realistic examples to make their point and are fun to read.

Two Kinds of 42 Rules Books

42 Rules books are published in two formats: the single-author book and the contributed-author book. The single-author book is a traditional book written by one author. The contributed-author book (like *42 Rules for Working Moms*) is a compilation of Rules, each written by a different contributor, which support the main topic. If you want to be the sole author of a book or one of its contributors, we can help you succeed!

42 Rules Program

A lot of people would like to write a book, but only a few actually do. Finding a publisher, and distributing and marketing the book are challenges that prevent even the most ambitious of authors to ever get started.

At 42 Rules, we help you focus on and be successful in the writing of your book. Our program concentrates on the following tasks so you don't have to.

- **Publishing:** You receive expert advice and guidance from the Executive Editor, copy editors, technical editors, and cover and layout designers to help you create your book.

- **Distribution:** We distribute your book through the major book distribution channels, like Baker and Taylor and Ingram, Amazon.com, Barnes and Noble, Borders Books, etc.

- **Marketing:** 42 Rules has a full-service marketing program that includes a customized Web page for you and your book, email registrations and campaigns, blogs, webcasts, media kits and more.

Whether you are writing a single-authored book or a contributed-author book, you will receive editorial support from 42 Rules Executive Editor, Laura Lowell, author of *42 Rules of Marketing*, which was rated Top 5 in Business Humor and Top 25 in Business Marketing on Amazon.com (December 2007), and author and Executive Editor of *42 Rules for Working Moms*.

Accepting Submissions

If you want to be a successful author, we'll provide you the tools to help make it happen. Start today by answering the following questions and visit our website at http://superstarpress.com/ for more information on submitting your 42 Rules book idea.

Super Star Press is now accepting submissions for books in the 42 Rules book series. For more information, email info@superstarpress.com or call 408-257-3000.

Other Happy About Books

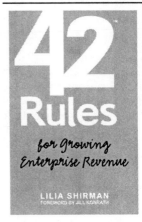

42 Rules for Growing Enterprise Revenue

This book is a brainstorming tool meant to provoke discussion and creativity within executive teams who are looking to boost their top line numbers.

Paperback: $19.95
eBook: $14.95

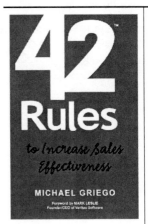

42 Rules to Increase Sales Effectiveness

42 Rules to Increase Sales Effectiveness upgrades and adjusts foundational rules for today's business environment to increase individual or team overall sales effectiveness.

Paperback: $19.95
eBook: $14.95

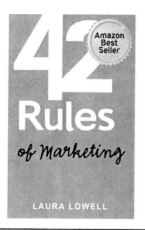

42 Rules of Marketing

This book is a compilation of ideas, theories, and practical approaches to marketing challenges the author has been collecting over the past 17 years.

Paperback: $19.95
eBook: $11.95

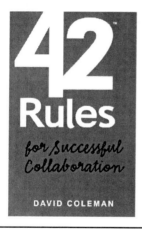

42 Rules for Successful Collaboration

Readers of this book will walk away with a much better idea how to be successful in their interactions with others via the computer.

Paperback: $19.95
eBook: $14.95

Purchase these books at Happy About
http://happyabout.info/
or at other online and physical bookstores.

A Message From Super Star Press™

Thank you for your purchase of this 42 Rules Series book. It is available online at: http://happyabout.info/42rules/prospects2customers.php or at other online and physical bookstores. To learn more about contributing to books in the 42 Rules series, check out http://superstarpress.com.

Please contact us for quantity discounts at sales@superstarpress.com.

If you want to be informed by email of upcoming books, please email bookupdate@superstarpress.com.

CPSIA information can be obtained at www.ICGtesting.com
Printed in the USA
BVOW031421200312

285517BV00007B/1/P